Remaining Reverend

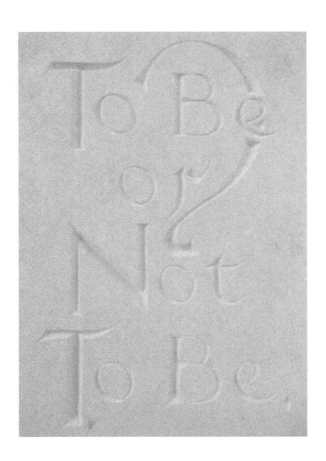

Self portrait

Remaining Reverend

Toddy Hoare

Covenanters Press

Covenanters Press
an imprint of
Zeticula Ltd,
Unit 13,
196 Rose Street,
Edinburgh,
EH2 4AT,
Scotland.

http://www.covenanters.co.uk
admin@covenanters.co.uk

First published 2019
Text © Toddy Hoare 2019

Illustrations and photographs © Toddy Hoare 2019
A Letter-cutting sampler/demo piece for Magdalen College School Arts Festival, July 2015, at Oxford Castle by Toddy Hoare on page 1 © Toddy Hoare 2019
Picture and article on page 110 © Oxford Mail 24 January 1979 used with permission.

ISBN 978-1-905022-37-3

A Te Deum to the glorious company of congregations, the goodly fellowship of vergers, the noble army of churchwardens and all whom I have served in those many capacities as priest and chaplain, or merely encouraged.

Acknowledgements

For a volume that Tony Russell, lately Bishop of Ely, said should be an historical document in 100 years, I acknowledge a cohort of people who have encouraged, moulded, guided and inspired as well as sharing my own spiritual journey.

No acknowledgement would be complete without my heartfelt thanks to the late Roger and the late Gaynor Kingdon for the generous use of their studio in Borrowby which made sabbatical projects possible, along with sermons in bronze, and other sculpture used in my ministry. Also to Peter Dennis for the availability always of a horse for hunting.

Most of all, I lovingly and with admiration acknowledge my family without whom ministry would have been very different, but I deliberately leave them out of these reflections as parish ministry is intrusive enough into life in the vicarage and their doings. Our labradors over the years played their parts too.

Contents

Time-line

Illustrations

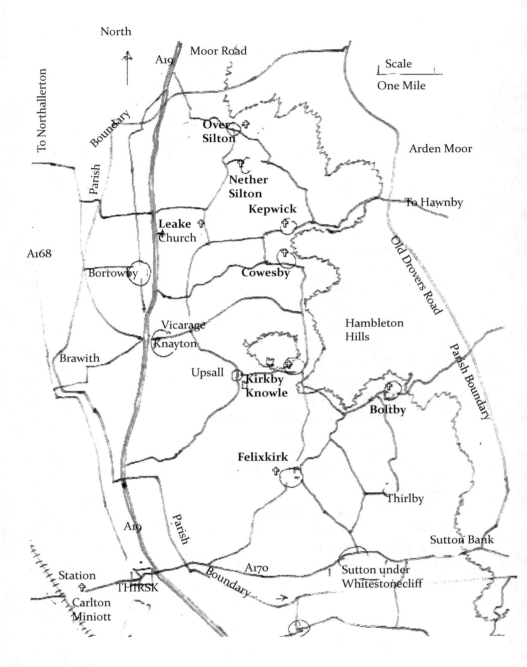

The eight parishes

In the beginning

In my time as a rural parish priest I signed more gun licences than conducted baptisms. Though the former did have to be renewed every five years, families did not present me with a new arrival every five years or sooner as the old registers suggested. However by the time I retired, I was marrying those I had baptised at the beginning of my ministry, on the edge of the North Yorkshire Moors.

Rural ministry is very rarely about growth, though I do remember one Archdeacon — on perusing the eternal annual returns of attendance — remarking that there was growth as the numbers were stable, despite a number of funerals.

Meanwhile the registers yielded other gems from Victorian times, when they were most filled in:

The — virtually annual — baptism of a new baby to one family in Thirlby showed the father's progress from *Farm Labourer* to *Engineman* to *Traction Engine & Thresher owner* (today's contractor) to *Farmer* (and therefore farm owner in his own right). Not a lot has changed where a man starts as a labourer, becomes an agricultural contractor and finishes farming his own and rented land. It is down to dedication and hard work.

It had been pointed out, on my arrival, that there were as many cows as ever there had been, but they were now divided amongst fewer owners. That means that the numbers of single house cows had shrunk but that as a whole they had become dairy herds of 30 head upwards.

Following foot and mouth disease (not served well by an inexperienced Department for Environment, Food and

Rural Affairs, with little overall knowledge and experience of practical farming, they should at least have employed those who had farm experience — which farmers would willingly give them) the number of herds decreased while the number of beasts in individual herds increased.

I remember one funeral wake at what had been a former farm. The farmer from Home Farm, next door, remarked that a new farmer to the district, years before, had asked why his cattle stripped the bark from the trees. He was told they needed more minerals; copper, especially, was lacking in the spring water, so he should buy a lick for his beasts. Some weeks later he asked again why the same cattle appeared not to prosper. Put some minerals in their feed, he was told. After a few more weeks the question was repeated; the new farmer was told he would need to get the vet in (i.e. the partnership of Siegfried and Herriot) to give the cattle a mineral injection to boost their welfare.

Next, they were dead. He would not invest in his cattle more than what he paid for them. Reads a bit like a fairy story but only the vet at the last might have waved a magic wand!

Home Farm was in the second generation of ownership after one of the local estates had to sell land to pay bills. I always enjoyed the farmer's wisdom. Nothing was bought on a loan. Sheep always recognised his old coat when he went to shepherd, feed or move them. For him the 'set aside' of the time was a disgrace, "A bad advert for farmers when elsewhere people are crying out for food." He would willingly have kept fields ticking over at cost for the corn to go as aid, more so as set aside often increased the work in getting those fields back into production that did not fallow more naturally. As I had my own grey Fergie he once employed me to harrow or roll some pasture. At various stages of my life I have covered most aspects of

St Felix, Felixkirk

Holy Trinity, Boltby

farming — and for longer periods when unemployed — so here was another string to that bow. Another time I was given a lesson, by a lady farmer, on doing sheep's bottoms and feet.

The number of hunts in or adjacent to the parishes needed all the digits on one hand to count them; Hurworth (with whom I managed a notable day after a funeral and saw six of my eight churches from horseback) and Bilsdale within the parishes; York and Ainstay bordered to the south, Sinnington (with whom I had hunted quite a lot before ordination) to the east; Bedale to the West.

Thus horses played a major part in the lives of parishioners, as indeed did local shoots — as the history behind the parishes explained. (One year I had some splendid shooting; a churchwarden broke his ankle, so let me have his gun for the rest of the season.) Unlike Canon Kyle [1] I had more than one parish and did not own farms within my parish so both to hunt and to shoot was impossible though a good way to meet many parishioners!

The North Riding did not generate a lot of income like the West Riding; instead those who made money in the latter and beyond came to the area to spend it, buying an estate and enjoying the traditional country sports. Hartlepool before World War I had the highest average income per capita in the country, mainly from the carrying trade with the Baltic states, but two estate villages had been bought by two brothers who cast cannons in Sheffield for the Royal Navy post Trafalgar in 1805. Furthermore they restored, repaired, built and endowed the churches and schools encompassed by their estates or in the local village.

In the 1880s England was at its most churched and crime at its lowest. I reaped the benefits in that the most church fabric needed was gutters cleaning to prevent

St Mary, Leake

5

All Saints, Nether Silton

damp — until lead was pinched from the roof of Leake. Two of the three village schools also closed in my time, as local families were smaller and bigger schools within reach, or by expanding Knayton to absorb Nether Silton, were seen to offer more.

Rural folk are forward in their thanks for what God provides, through their involvement with and dependence on nature, so besides Harvest Festival Thanksgiving we held a joint Thanksgiving for Fieldsports and Blessing of the Hounds once a year on or as near to St Hubertus Day in November. (The French do it with a great cacophony of horns!) Thus we would gather, usually at Kirkby Knowle, with two local hunts prior to a joint meet after, two local Beagle Packs, a gaggle of gamekeepers — both local and others from further afield where I had helped out — and as many token fishermen as could be mustered.

It was a good, hearty, and enjoyable response to the pleasure and livelihoods so many derived from the interest and opportunities. After a stirrup cup all set off about their respective pursuits and I continued the day as a fisher of men. When I returned home in the late afternoon there was a brush sticking out of my letterbox. To their delight the hunts had had a successful day so I was awarded the trophy. It served for many years in a low doorway reminding folk to duck (or grouse!) until "moth and decay did corrupt" the same.

1 There was Canon Kyle who was the incumbent at Ingleby/ Swainby and bought farms during the recession leaving the farmer there as tenant. Eventually he bought the local pub as it served the community. The then Archdeacon remonstrated about a clash of interests on a Sunday but was silenced with the assurance that it would not open until evensong was finished. For further reading, see *Forty Years in a Moorland Parish*. Canon John Christopher Atkinson tells of digging up tumulae in his parish.

St Mary's, Over Silton

St Wilfrid, Kirkby Knowle

St Michael and All Angels, Cowesby

Kepwick Memorial Chapel

Changing Times

My grandfather ministered through two World Wars, the depression and unemployment in between, losing at Dunkirk a younger son whose remains were never found, and the slow revival of the economy and social life in the 1950s. In between Archbishop William Temple gave up being a card carrying socialist and helped usher in the Welfare State of 1948. The Royal Army Chaplains Department ceased to bless guns and got more real, and better thought was given to what a just war might be.

After my art school years, and a lot more questioning by the Church following books like John Robinson 'Honest to God' and my time in the army on peace keeping duties in Northern Ireland, my ministry covered the demise of our Merchant Navy while with the Missions to Seamen, the demise of ICI and the steel industry in the North East while a curate, and the steady mission creep of the European Economic Community into the European Union. A full time artist after City & Guilds at London School of Art, recession in the early 1970s killed that venture for me, although sculpture remained with me and became part of my ministry.

In the late 1970s, while at Theological College, Wycliffe Hall in Oxford, apartheid in South Africa came apart; our coal mining and fishing industries were killed off, as they did not win Tory votes. Where my mother lived in the West Riding, there were several pits nearby, and I spent much time in St Andrew's Dock in Hull when sailing with a friend.

Within the wider church grandfather had the *Book of Common Prayer*. I had used *Series 2* at school with full Merbecke and Sung Eucharist and was confirmed at 17, importantly made and encouraged to think by Revd Thornley, the school chaplain.

The one mark of my ministry and of preaching in particular was a determination to make people think. Sculpture sometimes helped, based on theology, emotion and bible story. Before ordination we had a rewrite, *Series 3*, which culminated in the *Alternative Service Book* in 1980.

Not much mourned it was superseded in 2000 by *Common Worship,* at which point I found the parishes which I served were lost. With the co-operation of all we printed our own order or service for Holy Communion in a familiar order, leaving out what we did not want to use, retaining classic favourites like the Collect for Purity (from whom no secrets are hid), the Prayer of Humble Access (whose property rather than nature is always to show mercy) and the Lord's Prayer in traditional form with Thees and Thous in good Yorkshire tradition along with 'in earth' and 'forgiving them that trespass'. It meant the service kept a rhythm, with the aid of the rubric in proper red, without flipping back and forth, so people across the parish could be familiar and those who knew the *Book of Common Prayer*, which has never been abolished, would find some familiar prayers along with *BCP* collects for the Sundays. We also added a basic Baptism Service from *Series 2* and Confirmation.

Of Theology, Women's Ministry and other evolutions within the church during my time more anon.

Two Generations: on what was different

I suppose in many ways I learned my ministry on my maternal grandfather's knee. Edmund, like his twin brother Bob, failed the army medical in 1914, owing to ruptures at childbirth. Therefore he was unable to be an army chaplain. From his marriage to Myrtle Bardwell in 1915 until 1957, he was Rector of West Stafford three miles east of Dorchester, Dorset, with a Mission hut at Bockhampton. (Thomas Hardy once lived in the parish at Tenantrees before moving to Dorchester.) Beyond to the East was Morton[1]. My great-uncle Bob, Uvedale Robert Corbett-Winder — MFH of the South Hereford Hunt — went to drive French Ambulances.

When my mother joined my father, who was serving in Kenya during the Mau-Mau emergency, my sister and I were farmed out to our grandparents, so I did the rounds with my grandfather and helped in church on a Sunday — more by increasing the numbers than being useful, but I did take the collection at least once. Visiting seemed to be the priority followed by Sunday's sermon preparation, for which he had a double-ended red and blue pencil with which to underline various points. Sadly, I remember no sermons nor have any. He also did duty as High Sheriff's chaplain to Gen Floyer-Acland; another general, Gen Harry Smith, was in the congregation. The retired naval captain, Captain Crawford, rented some of the glebe land behind his house opposite the church to extend their garden. I would be sent down on my tricycle with sixpence to buy an enormous juicy peach from Mrs Crawford.

Sometimes I would set out with my grandfather on his visiting rounds. Mrs Baggs in the cottage down the lane, Momma White in the cottages above the village along the main road beyond The Wise Man pub. She always gave me a Nice biscuit, which I always thought had a funny taste. Halfway up the hill from the church in the cottages on top of the bank with the Post Office on the corner we would call on Mrs Woodsford.

I think there was someone beyond Mrs Hansford in the council houses up the side road off the main load on the corner opposite the pub and village hall. Mrs Hansford used to do for my grandmother once a week. The seven acres of glebe stretched from the Rectory behind the houses as far up as Mrs Hansford with the Southern Railway as the other side of the triangle. Grandfather used it as a market garden, paddock and tennis court. Now it is a vast housing estate from the early 1960s.

World War I forced social change. In Yorkshire, after her mother died of cancer and was buried in the garden of their house, my grandmother from the age of 12 ran the house, Bolton Hall near Bishop Wilton, for her father, but during the war she had to cook for herself. She took a maid, Lena, as the only domestic help with her from Yorkshire, to West Stafford. Lena married the local farmer, Frank Kellaway. He was from the Dorchester end of the village beyond West Stafford House, where a flag always flew if Sir Philip Egerton — who also owned Oulton Park in Cheshire — was at home.

Christine Bradshaw played the organ for grandfather as my mother had done, and even my sister did. Christine started practicing on St Andrew's, West Stafford, organ when young in the 1940s and became my Grandfather's organist for the rest of his ministry. Lena's daughter, Marion, married Ian Colman the son from the farm at the other end of the village towards Morton[1] thus uniting the village farms. Last time I visited the Colman farm was for their self-pick strawberries when my niece got married. Marion, probably then late teens, ran a Sunday school after the morning service but I ducked out.

My mother could have bought the Rectory for £2,000 when her father retired, but declined as she always found it damp, with the River Frome in front of the house across the lane. It was only years later when I was in the army at Lulworth that I discovered what good fishing it was!

Ironically it sold, about 18 months later, to a developer, who made a fortune from converting the tithe barn and coach house, along with the cottage and wood shed across the yard, and from building the housing estate on the glebe land. The diocese retained two sections of the walled gardens for a new vicarage and its garden, retaining the pump and old apple shed. Furthermore, there is irony in that my mother went on to run a market garden in Yorkshire. Future incumbents in the parish were the Archdeacons.

So what was different in my day? For a start my Hillside Parishes combined two former groups that each had had an incumbent. I had a choice of two vicarages. One at Felixkirk dated from 1660 needed money but boasted a coach house and tennis court. The other, at Knayton, dated from the 1930s in the old garth that had been given to the parish for a vicarage. I chose the latter as being central to the new group, although sadly nowhere near a church, though that meant there could be no favouritism. Felixkirk Vicarage sold for £60,000; Jan Ford of the Ford brewing family spent a further £60,000 on it. The diocese were slow tidying Leake and putting in new fireplaces downstairs so we as a family could not move in when planned and eventually had to live round the builders.

Grandfather had one church and a small community, while I took on eight churches amongst 12 villages with a population of about 2,000, three schools, and six village halls — not church halls, so I did not have running or

Wincobank Church

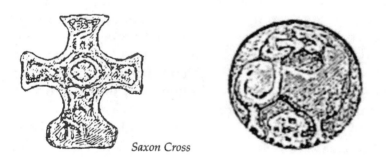

Saxon Cross

Saxon Cross and Mediaeval Beast

responsibility for them. There were five Methodist chapels, most being in villages without a church. By the time I retired there was only one operating because a single family largely funded it. The Roman Catholic Church was All Saints in Thirsk, the boundary of which enclosed my own along the moor edge from Sutton Bank along the Drovers' Road that had once been used for taking cattle and geese from the North to York and beyond. Two churches, Over Silton and Leake[2], were remote from habitation.

The most northerly church was Over Silton in a field below a terrace to the East of the village. The terrace showed signs of ancient hearths because of the clumps of nettles. Basically a Saxon chapel, with an enlarged chancel arch and a rough stone roof of what were probably frost-split top stones from the local quarry that had been used to supply stone.

The village possibly disappeared in the Black Death or merely moved when buildings became more substantial. Leake, the biggest church of all the eight, was beside the A19 beyond Knayton and below Borrowby. It was a twelfth century medieval building with a Saxon cross in the west side of the tower fabric and served what had been the hamlet for the Bishop of Durham's palace, opposite, with which the Jacobean Manor House had been built. Originally the living was in the hands of Durham.

It was a halfway house to York where they found his palace in Petergate near the Minster in the late 1980s. If the natives or others were hostile the Bishop could hole up in Crayke Castle further down the road. This was where the Scots, had they pushed on against Edward II, could have annihilated the English by driving them over the moor edge at Sutton Bank, after the Battle of Old Byland, near Scawton, in 1322.

There was evidence of a village at Leake but it had gone earlier, probably even before the Black Death when the ladies of the land rose up against their Danish masters and murdered them on St Brice's Day, 13 November 1002. Our gravedigger gave me an Edward I silver penny that he found in Leake churchyard. In the 19th century, before modern tests could tell us more about their origins, 500 people were found to have been buried in a pit there.

More history, more people, a more hectic age. It was decided when I started that there would be no 8am service because of milking, but a 9.00 am communion at one end of the group followed by an 11.00 am communion at the other end and a 6.00 pm evensong in one of the smaller churches, on a rota. Thus of five churches in use at any one time each got two services a month. The two-hour periods for the morning services were essential to give time to be with the congregation, even make a Parochial Church Council decision or do a house visit, plus time to travel some seven miles at most, without leaving one service early or arriving elsewhere late. One churchwarden did get the parish to make an earlier 10.45 start on the 11.00 service which was inconvenient and made a feeble excuse about lunch. I did prove I could get home after 12.00 and have a Sunday roast on the table for 1.00 pm. They gave up starting without me.

Felixkirk and Boltby were one original parish so in effect they had a communion every Sunday, as did Leake with whichever Silton was in use (Over = early Easter morn to Harvest in October as there was no electricity, Nether = the rest of the year with Christmas). Kirkby Knowle and Cowesby shared as a pair to have one morning communion and evensong each month.

Evensong fitted well with the priestly discipline of saying the office to make up for the impracticality, though ideal in theory, of saying the daily offices round the parish during the week. The fact that the group was 70 square miles in area meant the travel alone would have been prohibitive. As it was, only snow on one or two occasions rendered the chosen church empty at evensong. On one occasion there was only one person present; never cancelled.[3] By contrast Grandfather had an 8.00 am said communion, matins at 1100, but he would forgo a sermon if fewer than four were present, and evensong.

At Kirkby Knowle, there had been a vicarage which was bought by the farmer and landowner who had owned the other castle, New Building, in Upsall. He told me that when he bought it there was a tree growing in the big sitting room as the incumbent did not use it. I was told by my senior churchwarden that the last incumbent, Caesar Dupuis, had been a major shareholder in one of the many local Savings Banks in Thirsk. He never took a collection but paid for everything himself until all the local banks collapsed in the 1920s with the slump, whereupon the collection bag did circulate.

In fact the parishes held a lot of interesting history. Upsall, as in Upsala being Norse for House on the Hill, had an older castle with paled dyke that had belonged to the Scropes, still a Yorkshire Catholic family nearer York. On the hill above where New Building stood with some Norman cellars there had been a mint and an armoury in pre-Roman times, so it was an isolated strategic site.

Apparently the bit of moor that attached this island to the main moor had collapsed as the area was mined for ore and minerals and had engulfed a much larger, earlier Kirkby Knowle, of 11,000 souls as it was reckoned, so researches by Stuart Chisholm, the churchwarden, discovered. The knowle itself was an island just off the main body of the Moors. It must be said that Leake was also Norse for corpse, hence derivatives Lyche Gate to rest the coffin (corpse) and from Osmotherley to the north there was the Lyke Wake Walk to the east coast along which monks brought their dead from Bridlington to be buried at Fountains near Ripon.[4]

Other changes that were evident were social. There is a growing unwillingness in the world to accept defeat or another point of view. As there is much spiritual arrogance in the General Synod, so in wider life there is much 'Me-me-me' and 'I am right'. One instance was the move by Tony Blair to introduce a Hunting Ban. Nothing new, it was class warfare, but at the end of the day there was woeful ignorance by the antis, and a complete lack of understanding of rural life and humane pest control. I was therefore prepared to stick my head above the parapet. Having written a *Theology of Hunting* in its defence I was interviewed, written up in the press, spoke and won my case on *The Moral Maze*.

Then I was shipped up to Aberdeen to do a TV debate that was very biased. I found myself in the base of an arena with antis ranged all round me, bar a few supporters, including a fellow officer from soldiering days, now the factor at Braemar with his keepers. Two outspoken RSPCA officers could not accept that marksmen ever missed, even though I assured them I was an army marksman. I won the day when the one who was a retired admiral, if you please, asked if I was a fox would I prefer to be shot or hunted. Like a shot (forgive the pun) I said hunted, as there was a good chance of escape!

I would add that I was more worried about my trousers falling down than being in a pit surrounded by a baying crowd, as the producer insisted I removed my jacket as the grey Prince of Wales check confused the cameras. I was at least seated as I elected not to appear in my braces.

I won my case on *The Moral Maze*, with its formidable panel, on the grounds that death was no longer a daily event in a home somewhere but sanitised, as it was removed to an hospital or care home or hospice, so few died at their own home. As a result society was very far removed from dealing with death, or even the slaughter of their own household stock in the back yard. Many folk now can not bear the thought of the death of a fox, however humane, at the jaws of a hound or necessary as a pest in the countryside and a wilful slaughterer of poultry.

1 Morton is where Lawrence of Arabia is buried. My mother drove over to join the crowd at the time.

2 See drawings of Saxon cross on tower and roundel from wall illustrated on page 14

3 Once over the vicar of Kirby Knowle had the cure of Hornby over the moor in the next vale. One winter the churchwarden begged him not to ride over in the snow but he did, caught a chill and died. He had married a Walker daughter from Mount St John in Felixkirk. In the late 1980s I was contacted by a German who had bought a bureau in Bremerhaven that contained his old diaries. His daughter had married a German gentleman.

4 There were a number of monasteries within a good walk, Riveaulx and Old Byland who had argued over whose bell was ringing for the offices so Byland moved retaining all its fishponds which supplied York by the barrel load. While these were Norman foundations I felt that the Saxons, who were driven to seek sanctuary when William harried the North and left it at less than subsistence level (i.e. if any grew more than to feed their family the whole lot was destroyed), became the lay brethren in the monasteries and their different liturgy may have influenced strongly what was brought in by the Normans over time. It may be added that in view of all the fishponds there must have been duck, a useful food supplement and source of feathers for pillows, mattresses and duvets of the time. So much so that one northern abbot in London for parliament in the 14th or 15th century was taken to task for letting monastic life become softer to which he retorted that if the monasteries did not move with the times and have more appealing conditions they would not get the vocations!

Pastoral. The Post Office Thief

There were three Post Offices in the Hillsides group, almost at the three points of a triangle and therefore quite strategically placed. It was always useful to call in if I was visiting within the vicinity as I could be updated on news or if anyone in particular needed a visit. The local postman was also an useful source of information to tip me off if he found people out of sorts or stuck indoors.

One of the churchwardens took on the local post office in her village when the former postmistress retired. They had a charming little shih-tzu. She did not like me if I called in still wearing my cassock!

The churchwarden's husband was an accountant so he did the books, but was puzzled that, at the end of every month, the odd pennies would be missing. The amounts totted up. One day tidying round the dog basket seemed rather heavy and there under the blankets were the missing packets of £s in 100 penny bags. The thief was uncovered!

Occasional Offices, known in the trade as Hatch, Match & Despatch (or the four-wheel brigade - pram, car, hearse)

Grandfather abided by church discipline where practical, such as not conducting second marriages where a former partner was still alive, even to not marrying my mother as a divorcée a second time. In the event she was married in the Church of Scotland, which had less rigid rules, at St Columba's Pont Street. She was put off church when she took my sister and myself to the church in Bryanston Square, where we lived at the time, to be told we were not welcome - in effect excommunicated.

Having lived through this state of affairs, I was always prepared to remarry people, though it did demand a certain in depth interview to determine the cause of break-up and whether the person in question was a serial adulterer, wife-beater, gambler, alcoholic or whatever which might not enable the new relationship to flourish with God's blessing.

Such would be my decision, after referral to my suffragan bishop, which proved a useful stage to rethink anything if necessary. It was not without opposition from some members of the parish. Thank goodness that at the end of my parish ministry restrictions were relaxed along with residential qualification to be married in a church of choice. The latter rule earlier on in my parish ministry could be legitimately winked at by getting the bride to stay for 10 nights in the parish, usually with the churchwarden, to cover two consecutive Sundays when the Banns would be called. Often in the run up to the wedding the bride was not at work and I think it helped a couple who were in effect living together anyway to make a gear-change in preparation for marriage rather than continuing in the same old rut. In my mother's time it was sufficient to leave a suitcase in the parish to be regarded as "resident"!

Because Leake and Over Silton were by turn remote and romantic I did get requests from outside the parish for a second marriage but was able to say canon law expressly said one party for a second marriage had to be resident in the parish. Services of blessing after a civil marriage were allowed but could be hi-jacked as a wedding service with overdressed bride unless the liturgy for and the choreography of the ceremony were not carefully managed. The other hassle was the wretched photography in what was a serious ceremony. All had to be kept under control, whether preventing the 'professional' being on the loose in church and a major distraction, not to say intrusion, to preventing the congregation from behaving like a crowd of paparazzi with cameras popping. Thank goodness phone cameras were not around then. A further distraction I eliminated as my prerogative was a video.

I felt more emphasis needed to focus on what the couple said than relying on replays afterwards. A modern hazard is that many view much of life through a lens and do not see the wood for the trees they are lost in, so the bigger picture is missed and not experienced. I did make special provision for all to have their shots after which helped the flow of the service and getting bride and groom in the right position at the right time which all appreciated. Ironically, when I was a curate, my second rector introduced the idea of the couple pausing at the back while the congregation left, to much opposition. I saw it was not the idea itself but how he imposed it that caused the hostility, so I made it part of the service so they welcomed the wedded pair as they left the church for the outside world and it worked. That way it involved people and gave them a photo opportunity as the couple left the church.

As a curate in Guisborough there had been a wise old woman who was the verger. She had been a widow for many years but she was very supportive when I made mistakes and would cover for me. After one wedding she remarked that it would not last long. "Why?" I asked. "Because they were not with you," she said and went on to explain something I learned very quickly — and sadly would occasionally witness, despite my earlier preparation of the couple, to make the ceremony meaningful, and to an extent prevent it becoming just a film show. (I had read how one vicar saved a marriage by getting the couple to look at their video again, but I hoped opening their eyes would be better.)

The gist of Mrs Whealans' observation and wisdom was that where the service became a "Me-me-me" event and the bride, usually, was drunk — not literally; I had warned about that! — on the occasion, they were deaf to what it was about and just played at being the centre of attraction. However hard I tried, I saw the same portends myself, too often perhaps, and it made one's efforts seem inadequate on learning a couple had parted.

Marriage preparation was an important part of meeting and getting to know couples and an opportunity not to grab them for pew fodder but to open their eyes to the Christian faith so they could respond of their own free will. The old *BCP* Introduction to Holy Matrimony was as good a starting point as any, with many bible references. It was sad how few knew the Bible stories or references, even the wedding feast at Cana in John chapter 2 and the conversion of water into wine. What I tried to do was to highlight the poetry of the Bible and to try to get them to enter into the spirit of it. Thus to take the story of Eve being made from Adam's rib by God was not literal truth but a way into saying that each through the choice of their partner entered into and completed God's creativity on being bound (literally during the service!) together in Holy Matrimony and joining the flesh that God had divided in the first place, so to speak, when consummating their union.

Baptisms I found more difficult. Sometimes it would lead the parents to deeper faith but in the case of persistent non-churchgoers who could not even find a confirmed friend to be a godparent and stand for some example and future guidance it seemed a pointless and discouraging exercise. It might lay a foundation for another day but often those seeking marriage or baptism of their child had no idea if they had been confirmed.

I had found that when asked about a commission to do Jacob Wrestling, Genesis 32, the story itself set out the mechanics of baptism but which were more appropriate to adults. After all in the early church only the head of the house was baptised so everyone else was included, as was the case with Lydia in Acts and her whole purple dye manufacturing people. Jacob wrestled with himself: he had to come to terms with who he was, his relationship to God, and his relationship to his brother Esau, whom he had cheated, and was dreading the meeting with him. It was at Jabbock, running water, which he had to cross and recross (therefore turn around = repent), he was given a different name, Israel, and he walked differently after that. A very full description.

Of the occasional offices there was often a response that people wanted to know more or explore their faith without a then and there commitment to confirmation. I think there was only one year that there was no confirmation in the parishes. One major obstacle was that in talking about the symbolism of the service and the Christian faith, especially where it related to a story - say the Wedding at Cana - people simply did not know the story and felt inadequate so cut themselves off rather than admit ignorance. I can only blame the climes of the times in the 1970s and 80s when education became very wishy-washy over teaching any rudiments of faith or using Bible stories. I rejoiced when my daughters' teacher in the village primary school recognised how valuable and memorable were Bible stories and a useful grounding for the future. The climate of the day meant that school, despite being a church school, had an atheist head because it was more than non PC to ask questions of faith during interviews when it should have been glaringly obvious that a church school needed a head who subscribed to the Christian faith.

The biggest response I had to confirmation was in my first year in the Hillside Parishes because I could visit blind with no knowledge or preconceptions - a bit like a door to door salesman. Thus having banged on a door I would introduce myself and go on to offer what the Church could do and was anyone wanting to be baptised or confirmed? There was a positive response or at least an appreciated response. Some had been getting round to think about it, some felt their child ready as they had been "done" as older children, some parents even joined their children to be baptised and confirmed. It was useful 'catch-up' ministry.

What grandfather did under those circumstances I cannot say, being only 6 at the time. Occasional offices would have been few and far between with a small parish. I would not do private baptisms as the *Book of*

Common Prayer made plain but during a main service in whichever church so there was a sense of the parish and the church getting to know its new member and welcoming that person into the body of the Church. Even I had an easier time than when I was a curate with 20,000 in the parish. Admittedly one church made it easier to adapt to different services, liturgies and tastes, but then we could not for ever disrupt the main service with yet another baptism.

When I was single handed during an interregnum it was full on. The rector had set eight baptisms for any one service which was once a month on a Sunday afternoon. Where was the gathered church to receive them? We managed to get a volunteer group to welcome, act as sidesmen, and sing. Mrs Bendelow, the organist's mother, wrote a charming Welcome chorus rather like a lullaby to calm restless babies so there was a nucleus of the active church using the language of children. One Sunday on my own I conducted 18 baptisms in two sittings to keep abreast of demand. A bicycle cape was more use than a surplice with that amount of water being poured. Sometimes people had refused baptism for their child when we talked about it but at least they thought about it; I had more respect for them than those who came and never did anything more about it.

Again being single-handed as a curate meant there was probably at least one funeral a week and a couple of weddings on the Saturday, which also demanded respective visits, rehearsals and preparation. Weddings were a nightmare as the Rector allowed them on the hour, which I observed as a curate did not work; if one bride was late the next was appearing before the first left.

To add to the scrum couples who might have been married at the Methodist or United Reform Church chapels further down the High Street (Guisborough stood at the top on high ground with the Priory ruins behind

— so the lower the church down the street the lower its churchmanship) arrived to be photographed in the old priory with its lovely east end window arch still standing. When doing the marriage preparation in the vestry I would tell the couple the problem if a wedding was already booked beforehand that day and ask them to ask for at least a quarter of an hour later. When the Rector asked why was the wedding not on the hour I meekly answered because that was when the couple had asked for.

Funerals in grandfather's day were far more local and subject to local conditions. The churchyard was tiny and no longer used, though today more could be easily and tastefully added, so there was a cemetery at the top of the village above and just beyond the pub and village hall on the opposite side of the busy main road with a constant stream of gravel lorries going their allowed 20mph. Usually the deceased was laid out at home by one of the women of the village and the local joiner made the coffin.

On one occasion the winter was so severe that the sexton could not get a spade in the ground to dig the grave. The old lady was left in her cottage until the weather was milder, in effect also acting as a deep freeze to prevent the deceased decaying. Another time it was discovered when the last of the three sisters who kept the Post Office passed away that her petticoats were very heavy. They had always appeared to be somewhat poverty-struck, despite having a business, but all was revealed when the said petticoat yielded many half-crowns sewn into the hem.

One summer as sole priest while curate with the rector away on holiday I was faced with a big-town funeral as the manager of the local football team had died. We expected an invasion, largely of the unchurched, so how did we make them feel at home? I turned to Richard, our young full-time organist, as I always did for hymns and music as they were important. "Match of the Day", he said, striking up on the organ. It worked. Even at the crematorium the lovely organist liked a challenge rather than the bland C&A (Crimond and Abide with Me.) It needed to be appropriate and set a tone.

As a curate I had never been frightened of a funeral from the start as the first one I did — despite little preparation at college and only sitting in on one as curate whereupon I vowed never to do the same as there were far too many 'Light Perpetuals' — entailed having to push the hearse away from the church when it failed to start. John, the undertaker, always gave the priest a ride in the middle of the bench front seat.

Another funeral was a pauper to be buried at the far end of the cemetery. (I always checked where the grave was.) In the congregation, there was only a lady undertaker with her bearers, along with our lady verger, and the organist. I refused to allow the indignity of being wheeled in as if on a supermarket trolley on the collapsible bier that all hearses had within their depths.

I could only say that if the deceased had meant something to anyone during his life, helped someone or elicited a thank-you from someone he was as deserving as anyone to enter the Kingdom of God. Who was I to judge, and where was hope if there was not some recognition somewhere? That was not the end of it. When it came to carrying the coffin to the grave that area had not been mown: seeing the lady undertaker struggling I said "Here, you take the prayer book, and I will take the coffin."

Pre-ordination experience and ministry with the Missions to Seamen

Prior to training at a theological college I had been a lay chaplain and club warden of the Pelican Club in the Europoort, Holland, with the Missions to Seamen; tankers, bulk carriers, deep sea stuff and ferries.

One evening a seaman asked if I could bury his father? When the story came out, he had not died on board but, having been a seafarer too, he had requested his ashes were scattered at sea. There had been a delay while his son was sailing in the East and he was frightened the customs might think the ashes were drugs.

I said I thought I could sort it; the ship was to warn me and give a time and date when it would dock on its next voyage. I made 20 calls round the Dutch authorities as one department after another passed the buck. Looking at my notes I rang back the person who had been most helpful. Immediately he said he had referred me on. I demurred. When he grasped there was no body on board and no accident he suggested going out with the pilot in the launch; he put me in touch. Done and dusted.

My surprise was at the chaplain whom I had taken with me: we were given a cabin as a vestry on climbing aboard and there was the box of ashes which he immediately attacked with a screwdriver. Questioned he explained that a previous occasion the box had been consigned to the deep (still boxed to prevent the ashes enveloping everyone) only to have the complete box float and follow in the wake of the ship.

The other request during my time in the Mission Club was to field a request by a seaman to locate his uncle's place of rest. He had been in a composite platoon of Guards from Pirbright to form a body guard and defence when the Royal Navy evacuated the Dutch royal family during World War II. They had had to fight a rearguard action and he had been one of the casualties.

"Easy" I said. "leave it with me, I will ring the Military Attache and I will tell you next time you are here. Either you can get a taxi to the Hague, or I might be able to take you in the club mini-bus or 2CV whichever I happen to have at the time."

Easy? Not at all. Having been in the army, locating the Attache was the easy part, but he did not come back about the whereabouts as promised. I gave him a couple of days, then rang again. I was told there was a problem: nine men had been killed and buried at the Hague but only eight remembered. His was the missing name, being the only man from that particular Guards regiment.

Years later in the parish I was mailed the full story and told there would be a ceremony to remember him after his name had been added to the memorial. I had hoped to go but despite being a TA chaplain by then there were no spare seats offered by the Guards.

To close on this aspect of ministry with the Missions to Seamen I did have to arrange a memorial service for a pleasant young seaman, Duggie, who had been murdered at the foot of the gang-plank for some reason. No sailor would put to sea without some memorial service as if to exorcise the bad blood that must have caused the difference. On a more pastoral note I was requested to counsel a cabin boy before the crew would let the ship sail. I had a tight window being in Rotterdam that morning before they sailed about 2.00 pm.

It must be explained that there were seen as what were known as male and female ships. The latter worked harder because they were better looked after by the team of stewards, who were largely gay. They expected certain standards, like no dirty oily overalls in the mess dining room, and made the ship more homely. Rules aboard were simple: you may look but not touch. In the event one evening a middle aged steward minced into the club to join the crew. They set upon him and hustled him out. I went out to intervene and was held back by some, while others beat him up.

Outside the perimeter fence to the Shell storage depot, which hosted the club, the gateman could see a chap on the ground after a fight; an ambulance had been sent for. I was told he had gone too far and touched up a cabin boy who was rather distressed and would I counsel him next day? I would need half an hour, I replied. I duly arrived; having collected my thoughts, I talked to the lad to help him understand, forgive and hopefully move on without guilt or hate. After 20 mins there was the first mate banging on the door asking how much longer as they were ready to sail, four tugs were standing by at £1,000 an hour, but the crew would do nothing till I finished. Suffice to say the lad accepted what advice I could give him, the crew were happy to support him and ready and willing to leave when I finished five minutes later.[1]

The contrast with parish life was very different and pastoral necessity as an army chaplain more akin to ministry from the shoreside. In the Yeomanry we had two fatalities on exercise with armoured cars turning over and crushing anyone not down inside the turret as per orders. We had one cadet who suffered an epileptic fit, having had sleep deprivation on exercise, and I had to scoop him up and see him returned to Squadron HQ to be taken home. It was bitterly disappointing to him, out of the blue, as he had set his heart on a commission and enjoying a break from farming, which can be a lonely occupation.

In the parish the only funeral hiccough was being told, or perhaps rather not understanding, the wrong church. Undertakers tended to ring up that there was to be a funeral, burial at the church and details of the deceased. Come the day I had been told Burial at Over Silton. I arrived. Yes, the grave was dug; there was the organist who was in fact a nun, Sister Pamela, on release from the Order of the Holy Paraclete in Whitby — where she taught music in the school — to tend her elderly parents in one of the villages. No one else there. Time of funeral passed. Eventually the grave digger arrived. I said had we got the right day, to which he said yes — but there seemed to be a lot of people gathered at Leake. Hurrying Sister Pamela into the car we set off across the field and down the hill to the other church, encountering on the way up the undertaker who realised I must be at the other church. He had not made it clear the service was in the bigger church. In the event it worked out well and the family were both grateful and unfazed. The son, a headmaster, had not wanted to give an address; faced with a delay and silence he stepped into the breach to talk about his mother. With hindsight he found this most helpful. He told his story and all were better for it because it was personal.

I would conclude on funerals and this aspect of occasional offices as they where called that I would avoid spilling out an inevitable CV about someone I did not know but everyone else did. Usually there were others who knew the deceased properly and could talk about that person. I invariably introduced a gospel reading and centred on that as so few got to hear the gospel. Of course I mentioned the deceased by name. Heaven forbid that you did not but some, unfortunately, did fail to. More often than not when meeting the family to arrange the service they would let slip some gem, if one listened carefully, on which I could hang my words and if lucky find a hymn to complement it.

¹ The Church makes far too much fuss over homosexuality and needs to make more room for those it deems sinners from scripture, better understand the contexts in which Paul wrote, and learn a bit more about forgiveness from John 8, vI-II. It is not the church's duty to invade every bedroom like some moral police force from 1984.

Fabric

Eight churches, therefore eight plants and eight churchyards to maintain. Kepwick was a private memorial chapel built by the Warner[1] family after World War I. Their son was in the Royal Flying Corps faced with the Red Baron. It was therefore maintained by the estate and services were negotiated as required. Early in my ministry there old Mary Guthe paid me an honorarium for services, especially Easter Day (a fourth in the morning was a killer) which I accepted in lieu of expenses from the Siltons which were not forthcoming.

Her chauffeur-cum-butler would be sent down to prepare the chapel for me. It was then that I discovered he was a Berber from Morocco's Atlas Mountains. This did not matter to me and he was happy to do what he had learned to do.

When colleagues grumbled too much about their lay helpers I would calmly say I had a Muslim Verger who was no problem at all. As it happened, with his three children in the local and smallest village school, the intake was 15% Muslim which also caused amazement to those who thought we were backward out in the sticks. Funnily enough they enjoyed my assemblies for which they stayed and were better at answering questions because they actually listened. I used to visit them as a family and a prayer or advice was always expected. I was sad when they left the area as the boys had their bikes and they all enjoyed tobogganing in the snow. He was very pleased when I said of course he must come to the old lady's funeral.

When the Diocese demanded churchyard plans I persuaded the RAF photo recce from Wittering to photo them from the air. The Canberra that took the images had to tip on its side to enable the working of the camera lens, surprisingly mounted facing sideways, not down, which therefore meant not every picture had it all in. However I'm grateful that it gave me the bare bones (!), the shape and outline with the individual graves marked as a dark line. Thank you, boys in blue! It must have been one of the last missions of these planes as they were withdrawn from service not much later.

Having 'inherited' classic old English churchyards still in use with all the churches it seemed my charge was to keep their integrity. In fact diocesan regulations stated that headstones should harmonise with their surroundings. It was blindingly obvious that granite did not fit in with local type sandstone and limestone or even slate and I asked monumental masons to discourage what would stick out like a sore thumb. Of course there were those who wanted granite because it was permanent and did not weather. (I secretly hoped that this was not their idea of eternal life.) There were other restrictions and usually the diocese was way behind new moves in this area. Eventually I refused what someone could not have by diocesan rules, not as a result of my guidance, so it went to the consistory court. It was a hard lesson to take that the diocese did not support its own clergy in carrying out their express rulings. I argued my corner. The petition for the requested headstone or rather marker was refused. As a result, I had presented a counter petition[2] to tidy up the whole system I was faced with running, and won, though expenses were awarded against me. I refused to pay on the grounds I was only seeing to diocesan work. The chancellor was over-sympathetic to the mason who pleaded loss of trade but I knew that many of the granite stones were bought in as pre-prepared blanks along with other types of stone and were machine cut for the most part.

Graves presented other problems that had to be tackled. As we put sheep in to graze the grass it was possible to rule that all headstones had to be mudstones which meant that the headstone was one piece and 18 inches or a third of its length went into the ground to prevent it being pushed over, instead of a standard two-foot high blank that sat on a base and a foundation stone secured by a couple of dowels which were no match for a ewe wanting a scratch.

Also, space would be at a premium if we did not tighten up the siting of graves, so where no stones are in place on the older parts of the churchyard we dug afresh. Graves had to be closer together. A new grave had to be double-depth to leave room for a spouse, usually, or another member of the family. I was often asked to reserve a plot. I had to say I could during my tenure and made a note in the registers, but no agreement with me was binding on my successors.

I was lucky in my grave diggers who did a neat job, usually by hand, and had seen one dug between two old graves as if made to measure which exposed some of the trim as used to encircle a Christmas cake that adorned the edge of the old coffin lids. If the water table was high the grave would have to be emptied out before the end of the service and bracken or soft branches put in to act as a cloak to prevent a splash. I never had a grave collapse because of the wet while the service was in progress. Once a coffin was put in the wrong way round for some reason but the undertaker and bearers sorted that after the mourners had left.

Sheep did a useful job scattering the objects that diocesan regulations forbade that appeared on or around graves, like plastic flowers, or even a garden gnome. When complaints were made the stock answer was that it was against diocesan regulations so should not have been there. If they persisted or complained about the sheep we had to say if they were prepared to endow the churchyard with some funds we could pay to have it mown.

It was interesting to note that when previous bones were unearthed they were put in a discreet pile and reinterred respectfully when the grave was filled in, yet if there was work, on say a drain or cable or foul pipe from a new loo, Diocesan Advisory Committee rules stipulated we had to have an archaeologist on hand in case remains were unearthed. It seemed very unnecessary and greatly added to the cost of any work undertaken by the parish under faculty. When some bones of a medieval young girl were unearthed under the porch of Leake church I did cut a stone to mark her and enjoyed using QUINQUAGESIMA, a word no longer used in the new common lectionary for the Sunday in question, the Sunday before the beginning of Lent.

Church fabric kept better if the gutters were clean and serviceable, but ridding them of leaves in November was not so simple when churchwardens were not up to scaling ladders and no-one had a cherry picker. Often I would remind the diocese, as I do in retirement, that they would save a lot of money by employing a full time maintenance man to go round all the churches and vicarages and do the gutters. If there was no water streaming down walls the buildings would remain sound and less damp. Some hope!

The other problem was heating. Having tried and seen all sorts I have no doubt that a wet system with pipes is the best. If the boiler can tick over in winter and keep the fabric warm it is healthier for the church and a timely boost can make it homely for the congregation. Things under the pews leave no room for legs and feet, besides locking the church into keeping pews when there is a crying need for more liturgical space and room to enjoy other events. Overhead infra-red boils the brains and leaves the feet as ice cubes in winter.

The other essential was to support the churchwardens if they made an error. Here again their position carried liabilities and responsibilities. In one church there was a very tatty main beam, well worm ridden. Maybe, being oak, it would have survived another century, but churchwardens were determined to replace it and an ex pier-leg or whatever from Brighton, well pickled in salt, was found by the local builder. Now here was a job that was a straightforward builders' replacement. In view of architect's fees and the hassle of faculties, which only incumbents could understand with difficulty to fill in, the churchwardens gave the local go-ahead to proceed. All went well in the summer until the builder fell ill and the work was delayed having been started. Not a problem till the archdeacon decided to visit despite efforts to divert him. His face was a picture observing the chaos and rubble of a job in progress at Over Silton[3].

I had warned the PCC of the need for a faculty and the archdeacon was not going to award a certificate for the work with hindsight as being immediately necessary. We were all summoned before the chancellor at a consistory court. The archdeacon even tried to claim my previous unpaid costs but my defending solicitor, whom I paid in bronze sculpture, argued that that was irrelevant to the situation, which the chancellor accepted. In the event we were put where we should have started, so an architect's specification and a faculty had to be paid for. As a result of my sins I was co-opted onto the DAC. We had a good chairman, but I was able to bring along some common sense and some knowledge of my own findings from experience.

We had major work at Leake on five occasions:
rebuild the porch as mentioned already;
removing the bells and re-hanging them in a frame;[4]
in the choir vestry putting in a loo, kitchenette

and better facilities for a remote church to be able to entertain, with storage above for all the church clutter and flower vases, at a cost of £54,000 (which did entail a high standard of workmanship and oak at the behest of the DAC faculty);

putting in a wet system of heating;

replacing the entire roof cladding after the lead had been stolen.

This last met with hiccoughs. Firstly the thieves having cut and rolled all the lead (and the silver content of medieval lead was higher and more valuable) nearly got their lorry stuck so they had to unload some. English Heritage said we had to have lead for a grant. The architect admired the felt roof that the farmers put on. We replied we would leave it and renew it every ten years. If we had to have lead, we might as well leave it by the gate with a 'Help yourself' note rather than have the costs of further renewal. Then the insurance said we could not have the proposed stainless steel cladding without a bigger premium as it was more valuable as scrap than lead. Again we won the case by saying steel sheet was the thickness of razor blades and as sharp when cut, so thieves would shred their fingers. The stainless steel was painted to have a lead finish and the only drawback was that any downpour during a service sounded like being on a corrugated iron roof. I did get the friendly newshound to say we had the new roof booby trapped by the SAS so thieves to beware of having their b******s blown off!

Grandfather was charged dilapidations on his thatched rectory when he retired. I was saddened by the diocese cutting down the 33 different species of tree I had put in our ¾ acre garden, especially the walnut and mulberry trees which were just fruiting, after I retired.

1 I had given communion to Miss Warner (his sister) who had lived in Sowerby, when a curate and covering an interregnum in

Saltburn. James Herriot based Tricky-woo on her dog.

2 Roughly speaking it requested "that stone for headstones should be local, or limestone or sandstone, or slate (Welsh Blue, grey or Westmoreland Green) but not any form or colour of granite unless it matched a family one nearby either through the same name or direct relationship." There were further points made as to the area around the church that was to be exempt from granite to preserve its character which the chancellor did increase.

3 Over Silton was left a legacy in the hopes electricity might be laid on. However North Yorkshire National Parks insisted any cables would have to be underground, which would cost more than the legacy. The church benefited from the funds anyway and rebuilt the porch. The parish was relieved to stick with candles and I was interviewed on Japanese Breakfast Radio at 3am!

4 The bells were rehung and fixed so as not to swing and the rope for ringing went direct to the clapper. (Hence known as bonking by serious ringers when bells are stationary.) One bell was 11th Century, dedicated to Fr Aelred, 1110-1152, third Abbot of Rievaulx for his last 20 years. He wrote a masterful book *On Spiritual Friendship*. On the bell there is a story attached to the rest of the inscription "Father Aelred pray for us sinners of Greendale." This may have been where the convent was where the chaplain got a pretty young nun pregnant whom the nuns imprisoned, but she starved, aborted and the shackles fell off. On ambushing the chaplain the nuns demanded she castrate him. She fainted so he was spared that!. When the nuns asked Aelred what to do next he replied that enough damage had been done and they should be allowed to go. Wise words indeed!

Meetings, messages and meals

Never one for meetings I did have five PCCs as to begin with we tried to honour the identity of each community. By the millennium most wanted one joint PCC to make sorting and sharing easier, but at that point the barrack room lawyers dug their toes in, citing diocesan regulations, despite the then archdeacon, who unfortunately had never been a parish priest, saying we should experiment and find a *modus operandi* to suit.

From the beginning, having got the group working together, I fought off moves from the then archbishop and the diocese to break it all up and reallocate it, in effect robbing Peter to pay Paul. It worked so we got on with it and change for change sake was not going to endear parishioners into giving ongoing support. Some threw all their weight into remaining viable, others saw the grass as greener on the other side but never came up with another option. As a priest one had to work with those whom God gave you so it was only wise to stick with those who were helpful.

Even a joint PCC to speed up mutual decisions was difficult when blocked, yet I made everyone realise that if one parish wanted to change, say, the time of a service there was a knock on effect on all the others to which some could be blind or just plain selfish.

It was not, however gloom and doom. I was lucky to have good volunteer Parish Magazine editors as it was essential to have something encouraging and up to date information for the month ahead, and by the month ahead it meant the magazine had to be through the letter boxes before the end of the month before. We did hedge our bets on the calendar and go halfway on through the following month. Having able editors to compile a parish magazine and for the most part enjoy doing so I felt it was important to write a stimulating or thought provoking article every month.[1]

I found, again and again, the church hierarchy completely oblivious to the fact that parishes were dependent on volunteers. Many a time a diocese might issue a directive or lay out a course of action, often as a result of synodical deliberation at all levels, or compose a Mission Action Plan yet if there were no volunteers to carry it through the response was going to be nil as you cannot force folk against their freewill. Sometimes the same expectations are burdened on Non-stipendiary Ministers or Self Supporting Priests as they are now called. In the case of the latter a good friend who was a Diocesan Director of Ordinands would ask candidates how they were going to fit in training with the priorities of work/earning their living and being with their family. Good intentions were not much good if they cost the family.

I'm afraid I had very little time for General Synod or indeed Deanery Synod. Hot air, a distraction and too many briefcase clergy kidding themselves how busy they were. We had deanery reps on the PCC and that was sufficient for me as there was plenty of parish and pastoral work to be seen to. I think now, as I thought then, that General Synod spent far too much time deliberating on people's sexual behaviour. For me it was a matter for the individual who, as a churchgoer, had some idea of basic Christian teaching and values, so falling short would either lead to being found out and facing consequences or confession or mental strife. I saw no point in adding to an individual's burden, nor making that person an outcast. It was clergy duty to support not condemn.

Once I was summoned to a parishioner's house because his wife was by the front door with her bags packed. Oh dear. If only they had come to talk the problems through some time before...

Then the Church, General Synod again, was obsessed with homosexuality. It has always been there and many such want to serve God as best they can so let us leave them to live their lives. I do not want to know their details; I want to know them as people, as God's people, so let us stop pontificating and laying down the law. Many bishops over the years have been homosexual and sometimes the homosexual priest was a better pastor because he seemed to have a stronger dose of female ability to nurture than many of us. It seems as I reflect now, 10 years later, that the church is becoming more polarised on the issue and is more divided into party groups threatening schism every which way.

I was unaware of conservative evangelicals, reform and a whole host of other hot groups when I trained and little interested in labels afterwards. What builds Christ's Kingdom, not what destroys it, is important. Many years ago I wrote a service of A Celebration of Commitment for same sex couples; it was not a marriage service nor could it be dressed up as such. It was there to focus on and applaud the central tenet of the relationship - partnership and commitment. As naturally a same sex couple cannot produce children between them, it was designed to meet them where they could be met, and leave marriage to the focus of potential procreation, though I always pointed out to couples that the fruit of their union may not be children but could be some other benefit to others beyond themselves. I did make the same point to older heterosexual couples or those not wanting children much to their comfort.

I still write articles during interregnums in our local magazine because it should reflect that the Church is still alive and there to feed the spiritual side of our lives.

Having spent time in the Savoy and Hyde Park Hotel kitchens, whilst doing a course in Hotel Management, I realise how integral to our lives is food. I also realised all I had done before ordination came into play in my ministry - perhaps that really was being oneself.

While working in Holland as Missions to Seamen Lay Chaplain and Club Warden I would field calls from incoming ships, to lay on steak and chips for some, or — another time — anything other than rice, for a pilot who had been on a Chinese ship for some weeks.

So in the parish, during Lent, rather than give up it seemed more appropriate to do Food for Thought by providing a decent meal and a good speaker. Having encountered Clarissa Dickson Wright at the Great Yorkshire Showground it seemed she would be a suitable candidate to come and speak - not cook! She was good, though somewhat sidelined onto food and the Two Fat Ladies, rather than her battle with booze and experiences post Alcoholics Anonymous. Having known others who had fought the bottle successfully, though sometimes with two or three false starts, I had hoped she would enlighten parishioners - not of course because I thought them alcoholics!

Food was easier. At that time of year it was the end of the shooting season, or a time when keepers had to cull some of their cock pheasants, so there was meat for the asking to roast, carve and casserole. I felt it was only fair that as the priest behind the idea I should cook at least one evening.

Over the course of a few years we had a variety of speakers: William Dalrymple, the author, Ann Loades, a theologian from Durham University, the Abbot of Ampleforth or one of the monks, Sister Agatha[2] from the Bar Convent or else sometimes looking at issues that the parish wanted to engage or grapple with. This included some interfaith speakers and the Muslim apologists that were suggested were excellent and remained in touch.

Sadly I struck a duff draw with a couple of Jewish speakers who were very bigoted and I made a point of forgetting to ask their return when a Muslim speaker addressed us. Prior to this venture some of us made the effort to get to Durham to hear Bishop David Jenkins during Lent.

I did find that some parishioners could not accept that such occasions were meant to be both spiritually stimulating at that time of year and a gentle boost to parish funds. Given that the food was provided, the cost of a meal was less than a pub supper so the charge to each person was no more than a good night out and they brought their own wine. You cannot please all the people all the time but I was certainly not running the whole undertaking at a loss!

Once when visiting early on in my parish ministry a widower, known as Joiner Smith, expressed a lack of opportunity to go out and meet people which led to inaugurating an annual post Christmas parish lunch. Ticket prices had to be set to what our in-house caterer could manage, besides being her help to the parishes, but there was the usual nightmare of getting punters and their money by the deadline, with no cases of hardship to subsidise.

A small digression on rural hardship at this point reminds me of an encounter at Roger's Nursery at Pickering on an apple recognition day. I had gone wanting to identify and understand the apple trees in the vicarage garden. It had once been a garth, an orchard, having as I supposed Bramley apples for cooking.

The local variety was Knayton Apples, named after the village, because before World War II the area had been known as the Evesham of the north. Ample supplies of cooking apples were sent to Leeds market, no doubt via

Thirsk, where there was a junction on the main London line with a branch to Leeds via Ripon.

I fell into conversation with an old boy who said he haled from Bishop Wilton. I told him that my great-grandparents were buried there. He said that he remembered being sent, when a boy, by his mother to the vicarage to collect 2/6 for a Christmas turkey from the fund given for the purpose by the father of my grandmother (who was married to my clerical grandfather).

He also added the fund had long been swallowed up by one vicar, along with the fund endowed for the upkeep of our family graves. The graves seemed to have disappeared anyway, save for the plaque in the church to my great-uncle Tatton who died prematurely, so it was said, as a result of being gassed in World War I.

I can understand that if, say, £100-00 was given so that with annual interest of say 2%, it might yield 8 x 2/6 turkeys. This would be swallowed up eventually with inflation so the remaining capital could only go into a central parish fund, but the obligation still should have been there, along with the obligation to tidy that part of the churchyard that had been paid for.

Another occasion of feeding parishioners through necessity arose as a result of the foot and mouth disease outbreak that heralded the start of the new millennium. This occurrence had kept several dairy farmers around the parish villages captive on their farms, to prevent spread of the disease, for a good few months.

Having received a grant in retrospect, towards the end of their quarantine, I provided a meal and a speaker who was himself a farmer and Methodist lay reader for some fifty including their wives, to give them a chance to meet up and unwind. Luckily I had kept an account of the monies, as a mean minded parishioner wanted to catch me out embezzling church funds. I was able to pacify the archdeacon, whom I noted at the time did not immediately stand up for his clergy before false accusations. When the outbreak occurred I spent the whole day on the telephone checking how farmers were and what they might need.

Food is important and in some ways a great leveller as all are welcome in a parish, not just nobs on the one hand or the less well off on the other. Besides it also reflects the unrestricted access to the Lord's Table. In the case of the distribution of the Communion I always welcomed all in the hopes that all would come. Afterwards often proved an opportunity to talk to those who held back to ask if they wished to be confirmed, or in the event of their being Roman Catholic to repeat that they were welcome to receive communion in an Anglican Church and hopefully more able to share as spouses or as a family.

In the case of children coming to the sanctuary rail with their parents for communion, I had noted years ago that smaller children often pulled at their parents' hands to see what they received, so I always made a point of offering them a piece of bread or wafer as a taste so they were included. For any who might be shocked I pointed to the scriptures where if the body is not discerned it is not the body!

I should add that one of the skills I picked up, which has ever proved useful, prior to ordination was the ability to cook. My mother made sure I had basic skills, well employed at sea ocean racing when not working the foredeck (Fastnet 1971) or more gentle cruising in the Western Isles and Biscay, but these skills were honed when I spent a year away from art school learning hotel management; I spent the time in the kitchens of the Hyde Park Hotel (bakery, soup, larder and paying waiters) and then The Savoy (vegetables, fish). Here I was paid so little I had 2/6 left in my pocket after paying rent. Luckily at the same we were fed; for 1,000 employees there was a third kitchen which, despite the same fresh ingredients and status, was able to ruin the food, poorer than at school.

I had an early part-time job delivering fruit and veg from a wholesaler, stocking up from Covent Garden, driving anything from a Mini van to a pantechnicon, round Mayfair and the rest of London to Esher and Windsor Castle (on Fridays) and Buckingham Palace, where the kitchen fed 200 and another 70 if the Royal Nursery was functioning.

I kept the part time job and went back to Art School, turning my back on slave labour. As a result I made sure my Territorial Army troop cooked properly, and later at Theological College, when the cook was off sick for three days or so cooked the food for the college. Church and food do go together — witness those who have come to faith serving others or being served, and, in recent times, the growth of food banks. Charities such as Oxfam started in the University Church in Oxford years before.

From time to time 'gentlemen of the road' or tinkers claiming they had not received their benefits would knock on the vicarage door. I never gave money but issued food or a not-empty gas cylinder in the case of any who wanted to buy gas for cooking. One gratefully received the shoes I was wearing. He may have just left Durham, and offered to chop wood as he was handy with an axe. I declined the offer thinking maybe that was why he had been locked up in Durham. Another wanted the cost of his ticket to Middlesbrough. Obviously he had drunk his fare so I set him on the A19 to hitch a lift and advised him his wife might save money on Terry nappies against the cost of disposable items that take an age to biodegrade.

1 See appendix 1.
2 Author of *A Nun's Story*.

Flood

We were spared famine, having enjoyed the feast, but there were floods. Since the torrent of water that raged through Boscastle in 2004, there has been almost an annual deluge from rain and floods somewhere since. In 2005 it was the turn of the Hillside Parishes, Todmorden the year after, and Oxford the year after that, when we moved. The blight continues somewhere now, almost without fail.

It was on a Sunday at Kirkby Knowle at the beginning of June when the heavens opened, during an earlier evensong than usual. By the end of the service the rain had not abated and the road past the church was becoming a river. The wall of water levelled walls and hedges. In the parish we moved cars and adjourned soaked to the churchwarden's house.

Ironically, I had been on a walk that morning after the service on a Diocesan retreat at Wydale Hall near Pickering. I walked past a notice stating that in 1911 following a cloudburst a torrent had surged down the valley, sweeping all before it but luckily with no loss of life nor of stock.

The rain continued steadily for at least two-and-a-half hours and 50 houses across the villages were flooded. Because the roads were cut off we had little news coverage, save someone trying to cross the road in Sutton-under-Whitestonecliff; luckily he was roped to others, otherwise he would have been swept away.

I tried every route to get home but the water was too deep. After I encountered one submerged car on a lower road that undulated, I made a point of walking dubious stretches first. I got as far as a friend in another village by which time I was naked save for a towel.

He suggested, having supplied some dry clothes, that we baled out his neighbour, who was faced with the water that was running down the hill being caught between the two wings of the house and rising to window sill height. Inside the house was still dry but water was beginning to seep through air bricks and up through the hall floor. I advised the only course of action because water would ingress anyway was to make a channel for it from the front door down the passage, through the kitchen and out of the back door by the shortest route. Quickly all furniture and carpets were moved, barricades erected, doors shut with towels stoppering them, before the front door was opened. It was a successful damage limitation operation.

Since everyone seemed to be covered by insurance and accommodation found (though some repairs took a good year) there seemed little the Church could do beyond being a good neighbour as and where appropriate. However when visiting I noticed many gardens were devastated, most of which were labours of love not covered by insurance. I had been given some money but who deserved it more than anyone else? I hit on the idea of buying everyone two rose bushes, which the local garden centre would supply on demand, to restart their garden. This we expanded with a voluntary plant bank and a lorry load of topsoil was made available plus compost. It seemed this might best help remove the devastation that greeted anyone returning home and lift the spirits with hope for the future.

While many may enjoy a walk along a stream or a river bank there is still a need for good neighbourliness. The flooding highlighted the need for concerted and co-ordinated riparian maintenance. Some farmers and others whose property backed on to a stream or river would clear the banks and keep the channel flowing. Others did not bother and left the waterway to nature, which was fine until it clogged. The combination of the two differing approaches meant there were some stretches of fast flowing water then there was a damming effect caused by debris. In these situations the water built up behind the obstacle until weight and pressure broke through. The resulting surge carried all before it, making water levels rise more than they needed to if an even flow had been maintained.

Exorcism

One day I got a telephone call. My name was in the telephone directory under both Revd Toddy Hoare and the Revd. Patrick Hoare. Also the operators knew that if someone called wanting to speak to a priest they could get hold of me — one of the advantages of long term ministry in an area. Would I exorcise the house? There is a Diocesan Exorcist, but I thought it wise to clarify the facts before passing the caller on and saying if she got no joy she was to come back to me.

The facts were simple. She lived in Carlton Miniott, where she had a children's party for her son and seven friends. When they came in for tea there were nine children. When she got them sat down only eight were there.

The address was in the old railway sidings. Now Carlton Miniott was where Thirsk railway station was sited, on the straight stretch of line between York and Darlington on which engines and trains did speed trials. It had been also a big junction with extensive sidings as a line to Leeds used to branch off here.

It occurred to me, and I said so, that years ago a child, who had lived and died where her house stood, must have been flattened by an engine shunting wagons and the spirit had never found rest. I knew a little of this world of lost spirits as my landlady, when I was an art student in London, was practiced in these arts of bringing rest and peace. On following it up, this proved to be the case and the spirit found rest at the hands of the Diocesan Exorcist. I would add that I was not squeamish about having to do it myself - I see it as a case of passing on to God those who have failed to make the journey or for whatever reasons are stuck in a place.

What is spirit? It must be an energy within ourselves. Holy Spirit must be a creative energy, much the same as that which works through artists, which is felt within. Love must be an expression of it which borders on promiscuity at times. This aspect is better expressed in the four Greek words than in bland English Love:

Agape, deeper than brotherly love demanding nothing in return, self-giving;

Philos, a more cerebral love, a shared common interest;

Storge, the parental love that has to learn to let go;

Eros, the physical, the content of the honeymoon so to speak.

Thus I see spirit as something of God in us that we can grow, increase or sadly stifle in life, so at death what is of God returns to God. God is a fourth dimension in that sense where we are re-united with him.

Musing on Death

What is death for mortals but a conveyance?
Take a new dimension, called fourth maybe,
Where we become messengers, God see,
Carrying our love in an instance.
"To see him as he is, for we (alive)
Like him shall be" to quote 1 John 3.
With instant thought sixteen we can be
Or sixty one. Might we see George Five
Face to face whose head old pennies graced?
I don't see death as darkness deep
But perpetual light, not sleep
Everlasting but a system interlaced,
Parallel without matter, increased thought
Added to that first Word that all things wrought.

Gravestones and Sculpture

I have already said a few words about gravestones in general in the churchyard and my efforts to prevent a black and white chequer-board as the DAC always seemed to be one step behind whatever was in fashion. However, as I was often asked to cut the letters on a headstone - not that I advertised, it was by word of mouth - I found it a very valuable part of bereavement ministry, as the life of the departed could be reflected on and summed up.

Also I could escape the treacle that was poured out that so-and-so was a devoted spouse, parent, grandparent and whatever bland words might be added. Here was an opportunity to say something for posterity, to add interest, and if necessary a bit of local history. What did the person do? Family and friends would know the relationship to other family members already or subsequently buried. We could tell a new story.

There are probably at least thirty headstones cut by me in the parishes and half as many again round the country. I had been taught letter design and layout by William Sharpington at art school. From freelance days before ordination letter cutting had been my second string to sculpture and I developed as he had done my own bold alphabet but combining a little bit of italic or cursive style. It was good to discuss what to put on the stone, design it on paper and when approved to transfer it to the stone, adjust where necessary and cut it. William always painted his letters onto the stone to be cut — as had been the lettering on Trajan's Column — and his style had a distinct influence of the classic Roman letters. He never cut letters himself, but farmed out the cutting often to students. He taught us the importance of lay-out and using it to emphasise what was important. His strongest criticism was "All shout and none are heard" so nothing really stood out. A cry that is so true of many aspects of life today, especially church politics and General Synod.

I was often challenged for more than just lettering design. There were propellors for aviators, sheep heads for a shepherdess, a yacht, heraldry for others. Unlike William I never painted in the letters after they were cut, either.

One stone I particularly remember had a lot of lettering describing a genuine parish couple born there, lived here, buried there and their activities as Chapel organist or apiarist and forester. It was bartering payment for the engineer who put a bench tested and therefore less costly TVR engine and a second-hand five-speed gearbox in my expired Mark I Range Rover that was invaluable round the parish. In it I could see over hedges and spot farmers to visit. Or indeed to tow things: on one winter occasion a car up Upsall Hill in the snow which the lady driver could not manoeuvre and blocked the road. I had rope, tied her car to the front brackets and reversed to the top.

During my two sabbaticals in 25 years I got three Arts Council grants for sculpture projects. The first was a series of nine panels the size of an average door cast in *ciment fondu* depicting the Call of the Disciples (four had those who paired naturally, Peter and Andrew; James and John; Philip and Nathaniel (or Bartholomew as he was also identified); Simon and Judas Iscariot, the Zealots; the rest as four singles with suitable symbols drawn from the Gospels. Thaddeus I made autobiographical in relation to my own calling as so little is said about him in the Gospels. A ninth was Mary Magdalen[1] as the First Apostle.

The second were eight bigger panels of the Stations of the Cross sticking only to what was written in the Gospels

Mary Magdalen

(not implied so Veronica, True Icon, was out with the three falls) which were cast in Resin Bonded Bronze. Both sets were on display in the garden and buildings of Burton Agnes Hall[2], near Driffield in East Yorkshire, where the spaces they were put might have been tailor made for them.

The third grant covered a Millennium exhibition of Prelates, Priests and People depicting those within the church whom I encountered, starting with small sketches in the round of my 15 churchwardens (at any one time) and Archbishop Stuart Blanch who ordained me. Part of the grants was that each time the work was expected to tour round at least five venues so with a borrowed horse box the Rover earned its keep and I had busy days off. The exhibitions took in St Dunstan-in-the-West in Fleet Street, Nottingham, York, Durham, Bishop Auckland Castle (for the heads including two previous Bishops there: David Jenkins and Michael Turnbull) Ripon, Newcastle, Oxford, and Burford Priory.

It had been useful researching the Bible and background for the panels, and a joy to work from and get to know and talk to bishops, churchwardens and others while sculpting their heads; useful too in the case of churchwardens.

1 I had also done a life sized study of Mary Magdalen based on a pose from Modigliani and modelled from an art student as the figure was nude. Nude for good reason - all of us are naked before God and though not the prostitute she is often equated with she was in a sense stripped bare when seven devils were cast out according to Luke. Thanks to the faithful local news hack an article appeared in the local papers which was picked up by the Times causing a flurry of letters. Those against the ordination of women said she could not possibly be an apostle while my reply and others stated that clearly she was the first apostle as she was the first to see the risen Lord and be sent by Him to tell others, those being the criteria to qualify as an apostle. My main critic was the Ven. George Austin, then Archdeacon of York, on theological grounds, but he admired the work! He sadly died in February 2019.
2 They are no longer at Burton Agnes but available for hire to parishes.

Chaplaincies

Yorkshire Agricultural Society

A visit to the Great Yorkshire Show was an annual *must do* if in the county. It was while browsing in the Sheep Lines that I bumped into my old military boss, Major-General Geoffrey Collin, who had interviewed me in 1974 prior to my going full time in the army with the 15/19 KRH in Northern Ireland when he was GOC Northern Command. He was now the Honorary Show Director of the GYS.

As a result I found myself the following year in my suit and bowler hat as Donkey Steward and Steward for Leading Rein Classes. The role of steward indeed began at the bottom but it was fun and an education; pushy parents pot-hunting for their offspring ('Sit up and look as if you are enjoying it."), mothers inappropriately dressed or shoed trotting their offspring round trying to catch the judge's eye, fathers in too tight a suit with a plastic buttonhole, and old ladies with donkeys. Along with Heavy Horses, Hunters, and Four-in-Hand none of it was a difficult task for an ex-cavalryman.

Because we were urged to look out for special guests and help I noticed the Archbishop alone with his wife in the President's Box so I joined them. I must have been spotted as next year I was President's Box Steward with a delightful retired Royal Navy Captain —although a little deaf, having been gunnery officer — who had much hunted in his time. As a result we looked after all sorts during the three days, ensuring the right person took a salute or Royals got their seat.

I knew Geoffrey's children from when they lived in the General's House, not far from my studio in Langton; my rent was one bronze a year according to my fortunes and my landlord's brother was married to one of his daughters. Geoffrey picked my brains the next year about appointing a chaplain and working out such duties plus conducting Morning Prayers at the start of each day. This was resolved and his local vicar, ex Fleet Air Arm helicopter pilot, took on the role. We worked out an order of service, found readers for the lesson, and got off to a start after the main ring bell had summoned those able to come. We started in the President's Box but because of the bustle already growing in the main arena we subsequently moved to the Bandstand near the President's Pavilion. In due course the chaplain moved on to be 'housemaster' as he described it at Bishop Burton Agricultural College so I was the next appointee.

Shedding my steward's role but not the bowler hat, it was an excellent way to see parishioners involved in the show or with a trade stand. Morning Prayer became very much part of the start of the working day with about 30 people. The pupils of Durham School, which had a Highland Cattle herd, played a main part on the third day when their herd manager in his kilt read the lesson in the Scottish Vernacular.

In the event of Royal Visitors I had to say Grace at lunch which led to a further exchange with the Queen who remembered the Grace based on a Robert Louis Stevenson poem that I had first used when the Yeomanry dined her in Newcastle when I was the Queen's Own Yeomanry chaplain.

On another occasion when I encountered Prince Charles in the Rare Breeds Tent he asked what I was doing there; I could only reply that I was one of them too. Through the YAS we were able to offer introductions to rural ministry for would-be parish priests across the county, not just the diocese, and hands-on farm experience from many farmers eager to encourage clergy to know the industry and demands of ministry. There was a lot of support for the church from the rural community, when it was not upsetting them!

Another side of the chaplaincy was master-minding the annual YAS Harvest Thanksgiving Service which traditionally rotated round the three Yorkshire Minsters, York, Ripon, Beverley, and Selby Abbey where one year we had a Field Marshall tractor in the aisle which didn't half rattle the windows. At one of these the guest preacher was indisposed (the invite came from the President who held office for a year) so the sermon slot fell to me.

When a leading Roman Catholic President, whom I knew well, suggested we ought to stretch our catchment and be more ecumenical we had the service in his old school, Ampleforth. To be fully ecumenical the next year I negotiated Holy Trinity Harrogate, probably the biggest Methodist Chapel in the county. Thereafter we went more local to where the President lived or to rotate more fairly round a very large county, but also from necessity as the cathedral churches began to charge so much. York did not want to poach the festival from individual parishes, though a previous dean had written most of our original service. The procession of gifts, produce and prayers was a speciality that we retained and expanded, which also meant more people were involved, especially the Young Farmers. We did not include stock, or at least not in the church!

One other highlight of the chaplaincy was conducting Songs of Praise from the main arena on the show ground with the Black Dyke Band. Many appreciated that we held morning prayers even if their commitments that early in the morning prevented their joining us. The night before the show opened all the stewards gathered for the Show Director's Dinner, I think started by Sir John Dunnington-Jefferson who always got a mention and had been my Grandmother's neighbour near York. As chaplain I had to be prepared for the unusual. This ranged from hosting special guests to the burial or rather scattering of ashes of a certain lady who had been the stalwart of the goat classes for many years. These were duly scattered in the Goat Arena and her memory toasted.

Queen's Own Yeomanry Chaplain.

The military was in my blood, so inevitably I was drawn in that direction. My paternal grandfather was in the 4th Queen's Own Hussars from 1886 and served with Winston Churchill besides being captain of the winning regimental polo team in India in 1899.[1] He had a column in the 2nd Boer War and commanded the 4th QOH from 1905 to 1909. Thereafter he was on colonel's half-pay, and from 1912-1918 had the same Yeomanry Brigade (229) serving in Gallipoli, South Egypt, Suez and Palestine before being moved, prior to the capture of Damascus in 1918, to France where he was wounded in September and invalided home to marry in October.[2]

My father served in the 4th QOH 1941 - 1954 (Western Desert, Alamein, Driving & Maintenance school senior instructor Cyprus, Warminster Demonstration Squadron to acclimatise infantry at the training school there, Germany, Malaya where his next brother in the Black Watch was killed in 1949, Chobham Armour Development school, Mau-mau in Kenya).

My maternal grandfather Edmund, turned down for military service, was a parish priest from 1915. His younger twin Bob, also turned down, drove French Red Cross ambulances under the auspices of some Eastern

European lady aristocrat and may well have served with Jerome K Jerome[3] which would make a good book *Two Men in an Ambulance*. Their father had also been in the army before returning home to run the family estate.

I left school at 17 and aged 18 found myself commissioned into the Queen's Own Yorkshire Yeomanry. It was a very enjoyable experience and I made lasting friends with whom I did much sailing or with whom I still shoot. This lasted through to 1969 when the Yeomanry was disbanded so I spent two years on the Officers' Reserve of the Queen's Royal Irish Hussars as the 4th Queen's Own Hussars had been amalgamated with the 8th King's Royal Irish Hussars way back in 1957. With the Queen's Royal Irish Hussars I did a tour of the situation in Berlin.

In 1971 when a new Territorial Army system was launched I was asked to return to the Queen's Own Yeomanry which had been formed from Yorkshire, Ayrshire, Northumberland and Cheshire Yeomanries equipped with sedate Saladin armoured cars and the Ferret scout car on which my father had done acceptance trials in 1952. This involved a posting to Lulworth and Bovington to do a troop leaders course.

In 1975 having gone bust as a freelance sculptor and not wanting to teach (thanks to the Wilson/Heath induced recession) I went on a platoon commander's course at Warminster before being posted to Northern Ireland with the 15/19 King's Royal Hussars[4] on a Short Service Volunteer Commission. Here I encountered their amazing chaplain, an ex-Olympic rower, from whom I learned that to be ordained one had to be oneself, not adopt a funny god-suit.

I had resisted the sausage machine of confirmation at 14 at school, but in my last year in the sixth form my housemaster said to find out about it without obligation because the system was there to help you. The chaplain made us think and had made chapel interesting and challenging while the director of music had made the whole school sing the eucharist. As a result I was confirmed at 17, helped take evening worship and became aware of a call to the ministry, so Basil Pratt in N. Ireland was a great example. After my allotted time of service and with a continuing future probably confined to a desk with the rank of major I offered myself for ordination and returned to the QOY. Then I went to prepare for the ministry with the Missions to Seamen and from there did one last QOY camp in Germany before retiring.

An opportunity arose to do a bust of Princess Diana for the Light Dragoons as the 15/19th had become on a successful amalgamation with the 13/18th Hussars, as she had been appointed Colonel-in-Chief. The CO as my contemporary was dead keen — as were most of the regiment — but the Honorary Colonel deemed it had to be an oil painting, despite the RSM remarking the regiment had far too many paintings and that it would finish up in a back passage.

From Holland, vocation took me to Wycliffe Hall in Oxford for three years to train for ordination. By then I was married and we had an agricultural cottage on the Blenheim Estate. I realised I needed to earn holiday money, but sculpture was too dodgy — although there was some work to be done in London, at the behest of the late Cecil Thomas, to whom I had been a studio assistant a decade earlier. I dutifully carved the two Portland Stone lions adorning the side entrance to 108 Old Brompton Road, now the headquarters of the Royal Society of British Sculptors. That was a one off.

The only other training I had was soldiering. I pedalled round to the Oxford University Officer Training Corps and found myself as instructor to the Royal Armoured Corps troop with the familiar Saladin and Ferret, though the QOY had the new Fox armoured cars by then with a

Rardon canon. This was marvellous as I got a day's pay for a day's work at Captain's rate. I taught HGV driving, having got a licence in the QOY, in the Christmas holidays for a week, visiting exercise areas and preparing annual camp for a week in the Easter holiday and running the RAC troop part at camp for two weeks in the summer.

In term time Sunday obligations at college did not clash with the OUOTC training as the troop leader got his orders to carry on. My final fling to finish my soldiering time, and gain the missing days for a Territorial Decoration was a last camp in Cyprus back with the Queen's Royal Irish Hussars on UN peacekeeping duties. I covered the whole Green Line in a Ferret which in January, with the temperature at Troodos at -12 centigrade, saw me thaw out from hypothermia in the Austrian section hospital. I did however see a lot of the island, where St Paul went and converted the Governor, and had time to write my last essays for ordination on the General Ordination Exam.

Two years into my curacy I thought about doing a Reserve Royal Navy Chaplaincy part-time, on getting a parish of my own, but my enquiry drew blank as that department was being closed. Almost the day after, I got a letter from the QOY asking if I could return as Regimental Chaplain and before the retiring chaplain finished so there could be a hand-over. The suffragan bishop said — under the circumstances, because it was my old regiment — it was perfectly possible, and he was one who knew the ropes, having served in and also been chaplain in the Green Howards. Thus I served a second curacy during my first, but with the Territorial Army.

I did ten years earning a second Territorial Decoration. The duties were to support the troops during annual camp, conduct the regimental service during the week/ end, usually on a Saturday. As Sunday was a day off for the troops I often returned to the parish for Sunday duties if we were still training in England — about every three years there was a major exercise in Germany.

I was not always popular with the Royal Army Chaplains Dept, as being a newly raised regiment the QOY had adopted the custom, like the Navy, of not wearing rank. We were paid by seniority and my previous service gave me 3 years increase in pay for starters. Rank was a distraction and in fact it limited the effect and postings of chaplains in the regular army as if a padre became class 2 chaplain, i.e. Lieutenant-Colonel, he could not go back to a regiment where the padre usually ranked as a Major or Captain to be the same rank as the Commanding Officer. Anyway we blithely said "you are one rank above the person you are talking to"!

The Department's deployment was a muddle, so with the advent of Kuwait and the first Gulf War I was asked if I would go to Germany, from where serving padres had been deployed to the desert. I refused, to our then Bishop's relief, as the QOY was in reserve and if called up, no-one knowing how much the situation might escalate, I said my priority was to go with them, not be stuck in Germany. Basil Pratt was the senior chaplain out there; I would have joined him like a shot had it been at all possible.

Chaplain's duties otherwise involved Remembrance Sunday services where there was no local provision, a service one drill night a month in the Regimental Chapel at Denham Barracks in Newcastle, Old Comrades Association Services (I once got a helicopter ride to Ayr), and whatever else the regiment deemed appropriate.

The Queen came. For lunch I had written a Grace for her. She remarked that it was unusual and requested a copy, for which I was duly thanked.

Another time we had Princess Margaret who remarked to me "We don't like women priests, do we?" which was the hot topic at the time. "I don't know," I replied and went on to draw her attention to the daughter of a previous Dean of Windsor, known well to both her and to me, who would be amongst the first group to be ordained adding that she would make a very good priest. "I see what you mean," was the reply so I reckoned game, set and match to TH.

While having to deal direct with fatalities on exercise, in the event of an armoured car turning over or other accidents, and conducting the funeral if necessary, it was not my job to poach on the responsibilities of their local parish priest, nor to conduct baptisms of offspring in the regimental chapel but again to point them in the direction of their local parish priest. I did however conduct weddings of fellow officers with whom I had served, and some of their family funerals where I knew the parents. Not an us-and-them situation, as in all cases I was on standby, if the system failed or there were difficulties I could not smooth. The C of E is very much a system where those living in a parish come under the care of the appointed parish priest, so where I did operate outside my parish boundaries it was with the permission of the local priest.

Options for Change in 1990 saw a demoralised and overstretched military. In the 1930s my grandfather, the General, had campaigned and spoken up for keeping a larger TA or reserve force. Post World War II it seemed the army was more specialised in my day and such reliance on larger reserves was misplaced when regular army personnel were not getting enough family time. There was a recession and likely job shortages for those leaving the army.

The army was too stretched with continuing operations and training, and the TA was not always well integrated with the regular army, as they were perceived to be less well trained and experienced (a similar view of stipendiary ministry over Non-stipendiary ministers.) Relying on the

TA as an army on the cheap is not very workable.

In the event, having served in both camps, I wrote a letter to *The Times* on the subject arguing a larger standing army should be retained at the cost of the TA, most of whose personnel had jobs which retiring or redundant regular personnel would not get. The regular army applauded my support; the TA said get lost. I went onto the reserve pool until I was 50. Since then, with further integration and reductions, the TA has not been up to expected strength, and firms are not keen to hold places for those who volunteer for full time service as I had done in the 1970s [5]. Such flexibility was better if the individual was self-employed, so firms were not faced with the equivalent of employees on maternity leave. "A prophet is not without honour except in his own country and in his own house", Matthew 13, v57.

The Services, like the Church, were a victim of disregarding their own guidelines. Official army policy was personnel had to be over 25 to marry except with commanding officer's permission. As a result many squaddies married young wives, both still teenagers virtually, so the army was saddled with the baggage, impedimenta and extra facilities for these camp followers. Sadly many marriages did not last as the couple were too young to cope and she missed mum or could not survive the absences. The excuse was that if the door was not open the army would not get recruits. The reply should have been to stand fast so personnel were more mature when married and did not saddle the army with domestic problems. This was often worse if the CO was a bachelor as there was no senior wife to take a lead on welfare and maybe the next senior wife amongst the officers was too young to take it all on board.

This was further illustrated when I did a study day with a retired Major General, Henry Wood, under the auspices of St George's House Windsor and we looked at community needs. This was more than recognising that letter boxes needed to have bigger openings because more people were working from home and more goods were mail order. There were questions of infrastructure and local leadership, which was not necessarily through the church with less parish priests in many rural communities. There was a wind of change and churches and church halls were rising to the occasion as post offices or shops.

We then looked at a particular sink estate in a village close to Catterick. There was a housing estate with space and a generous square of grass in the middle. It was peopled with ex-wives and children of squaddies, but very much in danger of becoming a knocking shop area for corporals. Most were on social security and maintenance but they were leaderless and with no-one to speak for them; it was a headache for the army, though. In short, anyone with get-up-and-go had got up and gone. There were no easy answers because the root cause was not addressed.

When I was ordained I noticed that many of my senior colleagues, especially those nearing retirement, had done National Service and understood having to serve. The modern generation has not experienced this privilege but rather expects to be served which puts the contemporary church in a less favourable light." I am among you as one who serves." Luke 22, v 27.[6]

---

1 *My Early Life*. Winston S Churchill.
2 *Dear Miss Walker,* his letters to his future wife during World War I, edited by Toddy Hoare, now published by Helion & Co.
3 *Three Men in a Boat*. Jerome K Jerome.
4 While serving with both the 15/19 and QOY I had occasion to have to look after Fred May, the *Tatler* cartoonist, and got to know him well. Not knowing my address his son, who specialized in painting cars and planes, found, when his father died, a letter and draft of a picture of me. I had been set to do his head when back from abroad, so his son, Phil, kept the

letter on his mantlepiece and gave it to me 10 years later when I discovered he lived nearby in West Witton. We also had Andrew Festing on the ranges at Castlemartin to compose a painting of the QOY. He was most excited by the regimental service at the small chapel on the ranges which stood proud like a cathedral. The finished compromise was not so successful as the Sargeants' Mess insisted on the inclusion of more fighting vehicles which was not Andrew's forte.

5 Subsequent changes to TA deployment include training in certain skills to be battle casualty replacements (true reservist!) and integration has improved with TA personnel able to be seconded to a unit and paid at their civilian rate if more than army rates of pay. Employment from which they are released is supposed to be kept open for their return. Some may see the change as a sabbatical.

6 There have been calls in Parliament to end opening proceedings with prayer. My experience with the North Yorkshire County Council was that most councillors attended and those not much inclined to religion said they appreciated the opportunity as time to collect their thoughts before business in earnest. Prayers are not confined to denominations and indeed cross faith boundaries too.

Belfast

We filed down the street in the Falls
Turning, looking, graffiti on walls,
Unpopular, inviting abuse,
Others relieved by authorities' use
Of soldiers to keep a peace forgot.
Rifles ready, not a favourite task
For patrols whom locals didn't ask.
Children had a rope suspended
From a lamp post but it ended
Too low for fun and ariel twirls:
I stopped to raise higher its knot
Maypole like for two young girls.
Having patrolled many a mile
My achievement was their smile.

Other Chaplaincies

I served three times as North Yorkshire County Council chaplain, as the respective chairmen were well known to me through the parish, the Yorkshire Show or the army. For the same reason I also did chaplain duties four times to the High Sheriff of North Yorkshire twice, the last of Humberside once, and the East Riding of Yorkshire when it was restored. None were onerous tasks. I kicked off Council Meetings with Prayer and was around for a bit in case the ethics of certain issues needed clarifying were I to be asked, as I was sent agendas.

Ditto as High Sheriff's chaplain, though we had no gallows to inspect nor to give last rites to felons; I was on duty at the swearing in to say prayers, to read the lesson or even preach if there was no preacher on the day at the county legal services, where there would be grace to say at lunch. One highlight had been when a Rabbi preached in York Minster at the legal service. He of course referred to the holocaust at Clifford's Tower and mentioned he was probably the first Jew to say anything in the Minster for half a millennium! Hot on judgement and mercy, I felt Christian forgiveness got left out, more so in view of the legal service, but understandable when creditors, especially the crown, offered Jews baptism or death if they wanted their money back in the middle ages.

My Grandfather was chaplain to General Floyer-Acland who lived in the parish and was High Sheriff. As he was collecting grandfather on his way into Dorchester my grandmother decided I should bow to him. After much rehearsal, I remember I was kept off school for that morning, (Hip hip). The sheriff arrived: my grandmother got the scruff of my neck, dipped me once and that was it. Somewhat ignominious performance my end!

Because I was an active sculptor and had lived at 108 Old Brompton Road when studio assistant to Cecil Thomas, it was suggested by the then President of the Royal Society of British Sculptors (RBS), John Mills, for whom I had been studio assistant before art school, that I stood for election to the Society.

I duly submitted work which was well accepted but turned down at the AGM on the grounds I did not earn my living as a sculptor. How many of them did? The following year at the AGM, John proposed I should be chaplain to the society on the grounds that as a sculptor I knew the 'trade' and as a priest I could visit those too old to make meetings or gatherings or who might be in need of financial assistance. Again pandemonium and what about the equivalent for the Muslims. Proposal rejected. Wonder how many of them were Muslims?

I also did day chaplain duties in York Minster once a month in the summer; this would also involve midday mid-week communion in the de la Zouche chapel and once a month joining the healing service with the laying on of hands afterwards on the Wednesday which the retired Archdeacon of York, Leslie Stanbridge set up. He had caused a ripple of laughter when he presented me for ordination by reading out all my four Christian names then announcing 'commonly called Toddy' by which name I was ordained. This healing service was open to all and the laying on of hands had never daunted me. Indeed I often laid on hands at a Sunday Communion for a prayer of comfort when someone had been bereaved or had a spouse or child in hospital, or invited people to ask when they came for communion.

It was with the same archdeacon that I had a very interesting study tour of Israel in 1988. If I had not been on pilgrimage there in 1973, despite the tail end of a war, I would have found theological college very difficult but I could fall back on the visual images.

Even the Churching of Women, found in the Book of Common Prayer, was not without relevance despite being in an age of change. There were always some who wanted to give thanks after childbirth, but out of genuine desire to give thanks whether or not baptism of the child might follow.

Families of some of the resident tinkers, or 'Sackies' as they were known locally, when I was a curate, were insistent new mothers were not allowed in the kitchen until they had been "churched" as they were deemed unclean.

I found it more poignant to invite them up to the sanctuary rail with their newborn baby during the intercessions in a main service to use this snippet of old liturgy, not all word for word but in the spirit of giving thanks, as a visual image for prayers of support from the community with this new responsibility.

Not every chaplaincy was successful. I was a London livery company chaplain for a while; although they were generous with travel expenses, there were clashes with availability alongside parish and family demands. Also they could not understand the etiquette of not barging in on someone else's parish whatever the circumstances, as some occurrences would fall within the scope of the local parish priest. Like the Territorial Army Chaplaincy one was backup outside their meetings and the business that brought them together. It is worth noting that in the 1980s some companies had become glorified dining clubs but I did enjoy the rejuvenation of their original purpose and the return of members drawn from their trade.

On other occasions there was picking up the baton again. Martin Ingleby was a neighbour and an active member of the House of Lords who started the Yorkshire Prayer Breakfast which was affiliated to the Parliamentary Prayer Fellowship. He recruited me as one of his committee and I did 10 years or so until our discounted meeting at the Orangery, Settrington, came round.

Funnily enough this venue was my suggestion as two other obvious choices were rejected: the Merchant Adventurers' Hall in York as too noisy because there would be a market below and York Racecourse because gambling took place there (though not on a Saturday morning, it was pointed out!)

Soon after when he died someone picked up the mantle but it was too evangelical perhaps for the great and the good of the county and fizzled out. I felt it wrong that such a great county could not field a prayer breakfast so I resurrected it. One of the challenges was trying to pitch it to be attractive and relevant but also to meet somewhere that would be convenient. Yorkshire is a large county so rather like the Yorkshire Agricultural Show Harvest Thanksgiving I moved it round each year and allowed that probably most would not come every year but a good few locals might. We took in Hovingham Hall, Doncaster Prison, Ampleforth Abbey, and Sledmere House that had its own chapel and visitors' catering. Certainly Sir Tatton Sykes was delighted to have his chapel used. When I retired from Yorkshire I left it in the capable hands of Charlotte Bromet, a daughter of Sam Smith's brewing family.

I suppose it had been easier for me, as many likely invitees had been on my list of guests when I ran the St Leger champagne tent for the Yorkshire Yeomanry in the early 1970s, though I must admit getting mess bills in and balancing the books was always a nightmare.

Women's Ministry

I always felt the ordination of women was overdue. At Theological College the Principal, Jim Hickinbotham[1], certainly anticipated it; he was open to women training for the ministry and future ordination into the Diaconate in my time. Why Synod was so perverse on the obvious move and could not include initially the consecration of women as bishops, which was in itself only logical, is a disgrace.

Anthony Hanson's wife was a Methodist Lay Preacher so we included her and one other Reader in the parish, also a woman, ex-nurse, wife of retired doctor, on our preaching rota with so many churches and services. Anthony and Miriam did a husband and wife duet to suit themselves. The point was that when women were finally accepted to ordination they were no strangers to the congregation in leading worship, prayers or preaching. It was a smaller step for the parishes to experience a woman celebrant. Anthony on his retirement was my hon. curate.

Other subtle changes overtook the church. The wife from thenceforth was no longer necessarily the unpaid parish curate but a colleague, sometimes with her own parish but not paid as stipendiary in the York diocese, which was the church getting something for nothing, even though they might have a spare vicarage to let. I do not know if there were insurance contributions for an unpaid working wife. Latterly the church has stooped lower, to expect a working wife to support totally a husband in training, taking no thought for other family overheads like childcare if she worked full-time.

I have purposely kept the family out of these reflections. Let it be said that wives do not find living in a tied house easy and in a Vicarage one is always rather in the public eye so privacy comes at a premium. Indeed as a curate if we did not get out of the house on a day off it became a day of work as people would call or the telephone would ring. As an incumbent, days off were more flexible so if a usual day off got hi-jacked I would have another day instead. Funerals cannot wait and weddings were usually Saturdays, and school assemblies needed to be other than a clergy chapter day. The vicarage garden was always the fallback for the church fête (a likely kitchen invasion that might annoy the wife!) but with ¾ of an acre it was an excuse to spend some time there. Otherwise the vicar was on duty 24/7 and the wife (now spouse) fielded the phone and front door in his/her absence.

It was a relief to have women ordained and on board as colleagues. It never had been a problem for me as Genesis tells us that 'so God created man in his own image, in the image of God he created him; male and female he created them.' Genesis 1, v 27. It meant there was a more rounded ministry which embraced the female inclination towards nurture. There was room for men to express their more female side in ministry and women their male side. What a lot of fuss. Now we have women bishops which hopefully will break the mould and set a trend to diocesan bishops knowing and supporting their clergy better. The male dominated aspect was stagnating into a stereotype so a shake-up is overdue.

1 See *Oxford Mail* article, on page 110

My thoughts

I used to be surprised by people who joined the PCC to wield power. Most churchwardens and leading lights in 'my' respective churches were genuinely helpful and there to serve, but some were outspoken and did not share a wider vision for God's kingdom in their parish, yet other members were not prepared to contradict them. I had noticed the same thing in the Territorial Army that some, on gaining rank yet not being particularly successful in business, would throw their weight about and rather abuse their position. Ditto with the PCC with those who could not recognise the need to serve. One such warden once tackled me for lack of leadership and I had to point out the nature of priesthood was to serve, very much as the basic criteria to be an officer was to serve.

The title of this reflection, 'Remaining Reverend', picks up on the fact that as a priest one does not retire unless defrocked. I have retired from parish ministry but as a priest I continue to serve where requested and celebrate communion or conduct occasional offices when called upon to do so. My successor in North Yorkshire had yet another group of parishes added making eleven churches in all but with a retired or self-supporting priest in the extra vicarage. I also do day chaplain in the summer or winter midweek communion at Christ Church Cathedral in Oxford (which is also the College Chapel.)

It was during these day chaplaincies that there were interesting encounters or requests.

On one particular occasion in York I was asked to bless a wedding ring. I explained I could not just conduct a wedding, so to speak, there and then but 'tell me more'. "Oh no," they said "not a wedding: it is just that this is a new ring because the old one was worn out!" Of course I obliged and it was very special.

Such moments for priests are special because you are drawn in to share very private and intimate aspects of people's lives. In Oxford I had a long conversation with two Muslim sisters. Both spoke good English, one had a doctorate and the other was on her way to one. They came from the United Arab Emirates. Their mother was Scottish but had converted to Islam when she married. We had a very open and wide ranging discussion for at least 20 minutes.

One of the topics covered was consanguinity which produced a lot of medical problems where marriage tended to be within the wider family, often for financial reasons of old, but this led to a rogue gene that affected the blood and eventually the liver or kidneys. It was therefore decreed in most of the Gulf states that couples wanting to marry had to have a blood test first. While the authorities could not prevent their marriage if both sported this same gene and therefore were at a greater risk of their children suffering badly from it, they did advise them not to have children. Education and experience were slowly making positive headway in a backward culture. We remained in touch for some time - such is e-mail.

St Brides in Fleet Street was my spiritual home from art school days. When William Sharpington asked me where I worshipped in London, I could only say wherever with so many churches to visit. He bade me come and afterwards meet the rector, Dewi Morgan, who was a great encouragement.

He led the 1973 pilgrimage to the Holy Land where the average age even allowing for me was nigh on 80. It was a gentle pace and I made good friends, including introductions to the British School of Archaeology and seeing parts of Jerusalem and Abu Ghosh not open to others. It was Dewi who sent a telegram when I was licensed to the Hillsides (long before emails!) "May the disturbance of the Holy Spirit be with you." Wise words because a parish priest cannot just sit back. We are there to stir people up and as much as with my sculpture when doing sermons in bronze or Bible study in 3D I sense a falling short if I do not make people think.

Residential training at theological college had imposed a not burdensome discipline of the daily office which was re-inforced by my rector when I served my title as a curate. Yes, it was easier with either time set aside in college or with the church a short bike ride up town. Easier still as throughout my schooldays there had been morning chapel every day and in the evening before supper at prep-school. This also led into prayer and study but not so easy to keep in a scattered parish. Yes, I would say the office and usually use the psalms. Bible study centred more round what had to be preached or researched for other occasions whether three hours at Good Friday or background to a sculpture or an attempt at Bible commentary encouraged by Leslie, the said archdeacon. I did away with a lectionary apart from Sunday readings and worked my way continuously through different Old Testament books, the Gospels, and lastly the epistles. If stopped, away, or at monthly chapter I did not miss out but continued from where I had stopped the time before.

Study was important. I rejoiced in a private tutor, Canon Anthony Hanson, retired missionary from India and Professor of Theology at Hull. Along with ex-army churchwardens, he interviewed me for the Hillside

Parishes and remarked I was frightfully nice but had little theology! He set about rectifying it with a not unwilling pupil. His twin brother Richard was Professor of Theology at the other end of the M62 in Manchester.

Anthony set up an MA course at Hull "A Theological Understanding of Industrial Society" which I completed in 1990. We had to focus on the main or secondary industry of the parish for a dissertation in the second year. I chose Shooting, which was a big earner in the Hillsides, and I had an unofficial chaplaincy to the grouse moors, having been there full time in the summers when I was at theological college and needed to earn the family keep. This was later published as a Theology of Shooting:"Beyond my Parish Boundaries" and I did a back-to-back reprise a Theology of Hunting: "The Wagging Tail" with a monograph on the theology of fishing, "The Catch", in the light of the government introducing legislation to ban hunting with few knowing much about it and even less real knowledge shown by the hug-a-bunny brigade.

Anthony was also a useful asset in leading Bible Study at the start of chapter meetings. It was a reflection on the reality of the Word and how often it was relevant to the discussion, and business that followed. As a curate we had had the same discipline in Chapter so long after Anthony had died (like his twin, of cancer of the oesophagus) it always enlightened the day the clergy met, until we had an unenlightened rural dean who declared we did not have time. To be honest, without study together, chapter is a waste of time.

Prayer changed too. I always offered the chance to share a prayer when I concluded a visit and was seldom refused, and other prayers came as topic or need arose. I did not do many hospital visits as there were hospital chaplains. I made a point of calling in when a patient returned home, if only to make sure they were getting the help they needed, and even on one occasion putting hot water bottles in the beds before their return! Yes, I did visit regular congregation in hospital if nearby and I also did prison visiting when parishioners ended up there. I was usually able to get a one-to-one room, but times in the big meeting left me wanting a bath when I got home. This had not been necessary when posted to a remand home when at college!

One of my more interesting and challenging requests was to join a group headed by Tony Russell (now a near neighbour up the village in retirement), before he became Bishop of Dorchester and then Ely, compiling prayers and services for rural ministry and celebrating the rural year Harvest, Lammas (the first loaf from ripened corn), Rogation (when we pray for future crops and the farmers spray!), Plough Sunday and some general adaptable liturgy as occasion might demand. Tony was based at the Arthur Rank Centre at Stoneleigh and Chaplain to the Royal Show long before its demise. I found I had written not a few of the prayers in the final volume edited by Mervyn Wilson. It was an enjoyable and rewarding experience providing an useful resource.

By request I would take Communion to hospital. As a curate doing the weekly hospital and geriatric round I had decided against reserved sacrament, partly because it denied the older folk many of the familiar words of consecration and comfort. As a result I would invite the whole ward and any staff with time to join in. In fact as a curate I shared with my opposite Roman Catholic number who would administer my chalice and give his reserved sacrament to his own church members. We were a good team but his rural dean was always pulling him up. Ecumenical one step forward and two back.

As a parish priest money, fund raising etc were the responsibilities of the treasurer and the PCC. Sometimes a clergy lead was necessary and as a curate I would do a shoe shine, being the nearest thing to foot washing, for Christian Aid in the market place and invite donations. Tea on tap, another year, proved not as remunerative so, with those clergy across the denominations who could, we went back to shoe-shining. When an incumbent I continued this in Thirsk market. Some clergy found it *infra dig* so mostly I was a one man band but unlucky not to top £100-00 in the morning. When there was a sympathetic newshound in the town who would always write up positive priestly or parish activities he got the RSM from the nearby garrison to march down a platoon of volunteers for a brush up. It was good banter; having as an art student earned money in Covent Garden Market as a delivery driver it was second nature.

With the help of the same newshound we tried to draw attention to re-cycling, especially aluminium cans. He timed me to see how many when set up I could stamp flat in a minute. It was about 39, duly photographed and written up; however, the exploit was turned down by the Guinness Book of Records as no such entry previously existed!

Having been raised a Christian and schooled as such I had found it hard when posted to where I live now on a college visit in Lent to give a testimony when others recounted their conversion experiences. I could only say that I was born and raised a Christian, had followed my Grandfather, been a Lay Chaplain in Holland for the Missions to Seamen and all that I had done to date seemed to come into play in my ministry to date and training. That was to continue. However it was encouraging when a couple said afterwards they were glad I had normal roots too!

Having always thought I would stay in harness until 71 and eligible for a full pension, I found that when I retired a decade earlier I did not realise how tired I was, even near burn-out like Elijah, when he took to Mount Horeb and was asked what was he doing there until he listened to the utter silence and heard God, I Kings 19.

So when Liz, my wife, got a job she could not refuse in Oxford at my old college teaching Spiritual Formation I took early retirement. Not a complete full pension but just before it was calculated over a longer period of service. I was offered several House for Duty posts but retirement was retirement with no obligations and the freedom to see grandchildren at week-ends. Ministry did not come to a full stop but it was a relief to have no work pressure, to be house-husband and cook, and try my hand at a bit more sculpture, as we had space for that while the farm buildings round our house were not required. 10 years of various exhibitions were fruitless but I did get some commissions and letter cutting.

Encouragement was more often there than not in those 25 years as parish priest. At college we had the wisdom of Bishop Stephen Neill, who taught us church history; I quipped he merely opened his diary being 80 then. I had a good friend in my training incumbent, Robert Gibson, and of course Anthony Hanson to keep my reading up to date. Over the years I met and stayed in touch with others and by regular correspondence with Bishop Kenneth Riches, whom I got to know as he lived in Dunwich, where St Felix, patron saint of Felixkirk, was bishop and we wanted a preacher at a patronal festival. Often he would complain of the *accidie* in the church, a good Chaucerian word, but we had to admit that however much the Church annoyed us we still loved her. I still have his letters.

Another correspondent, whom I met in Jerusalem was Revd Joe Bishop, an American who had been a World War II chaplain in their Navy; never to refuse a challenge in retirement, he set up an Aids hospice where his stepson died in his arms. He buried three wives, but I only met his second wife. He sponsored a sculpture exhibition of my work which went from Stonington near where he lived, to Washington DC in Georgetown parish, to New York Cathedral, St John the Divine, where I administered the biggest chalice I have ever held - like a soup tureen.

I was lucky enough in that the RAF on their weekly transport flight were able to take the two packing cases of sculpture there and back and when they got stuck in customs across the pond a fellow officer from 15/19 days and then a Military Attache was able to pull rank and get it sorted. The husband of the parish secretary in Washington was a submarine captain and he had managed to get the packages released in the first place. It was the first foray of Prelates, Priests and People and a few other items expressing theology that I had started to do. As a thank you Joe commissioned me to do a study of Jacob Wrestling[1.]

I do not subscribe to angels so he was amazed to find no wings but came to appreciate the insight more.

I was asked by the grand-daughter of a widow, whose husband I had buried early on after my arrival in the Hillsides, to read her dissertation on Fashion for her Art School degree as she knew I had been to art school. As it happened I had just completed a figure as my take on the fashion industry. My nieces also worked in fashion and my daughters had done a day's modelling for Laura Ashley through their cousin. Funnily enough I had just read a book on the theology of clothing and fashion by someone now ordained who started in the "rag trade" as Eric Newby called it. I made some corrections and suggestions; she commented I knew more about fashion than her tutor!

A final reflection

I have been asked to fill in the occasional questionnaire. Throughout my ministry there was gradual change which kept it interesting. When I first had a parish, I noticed that as time went on older priests were less inclined to go to clergy meetings and deanery synods, diocesan conferences and the like; I think often because they merely wanted to get on with their own parish ministry and not join in re-inventing the wheel once more. Clergy are not managers, nor called to be: they have laity to help. Clergy are hopeless at delegating which is an aspect of management but nor are they indispensable, and nor can they do it all. They need to learn where and when to say No.

I have three concerns about clergy in the Church of England:

1. Briefcase Clergy. We are not managers; we should be pastors. Too much bureaucracy and rushing off to meetings to be busy. The laity are quite capable of managing the plant and should be encouraged. More training and encouragement needed for the noble army of churchwardens. I deplore Welby's sending clergy or some, earmarked too soon, off on management courses. We are not C of E PLC. Each bishop is a Shepherd of Shepherds not a corporation manager.

2. Ambitious clergy. Where is the sense of vocation? Should not bishops know their clergy better from training onwards and place them as they deem their skills to meet what needs to be done. Too many clerics see it as a career with boxes to tick for advancement. If cherry-picked too soon it could lead to disappointment.

3. Untrained clergy. I am concerned that the new trend towards part-time training will not ground ordinands in spiritual formation which is the strength of residential training. Furthermore there is too much emphasis on peripheries at the expense of knowing and understanding the NT and the point of view of others who may not be so fundamental for instance. The Church has become too like political parties, especially at Synod.

If there is to be a future for parish ministry then pastoral care (feeding, teaching, preaching, supporting) and serving need to be the priority. Visiting is less easy than in my ministry days and my grandfather's as few parishioners are at home by day and evenings are occupied with many other activities that may or may not be of parish origin. There may be a Minster model where a whole lot of rural parishes are grouped together under a team, when hopefully some members are delegated to a parish group within what really is still the deanery and they would live in the local vicarages but their other skills are to be used more widely in the group. Hopefully within the group one of the number will have had a serious grounding in theology and be able to lead and mastermind local study and bible courses for parishioners. Within the group there will have to be greater ability to support what happens where it takes place and some churches will have to focus on special events and festivals for their own services and continuity.

As my grandfather had a watchword for his ministry to 'live this day as if t'were thy last' mine would be from Psalm 36 v9: "O Lord, in thy light may we see light." Incidentally the Wycliffe motto on the lectern in chapel is a variation "The entrance of thy words giveth light" Psalm 119, v 130. A useful reminder for any preacher though that lectern arrived after my time!

Stabat Mater

There stands his mother, hesitant, short of breath,
Supported afar off in her anguish by others
As her son, who once snoozed upon her breast
When a babe taking a nourished rest,
Now dies a lingering terrorist's death,
That they in turn mete out vile brothers
To those of a different persuasion.
His crucified body on his deposition
Will have a final maternal embrace
With kisses on his disfigured face
Actions as sharp as piercing sword.
Your grief is ours for one adored.
Where in such sorrow can grace reside
Escaping death's dominion that love abide?

Spiritual Reflection

Disconnected, the mind needs space
To find equilibrium. Reflection
Leads to Inner calm and peace
Offering confidence and reconciliation
By reviewing faith and identity.
Who am I, where am I going, what are my strengths?
Confronting self opens, removes pity,
Truth has power to rightfully predict
Able to face those who go to any lengths
To confound, confuse and contradict
Raising the individual above rejection.
Experiencing all humiliation
Jesus man's spiritual depths plumbed
That individuals to no worse succumbed.

My love for Jesus remains as man to man
AGAPE rather than EROS
But to the Holy Spirit it's answering
To her call as man to woman.
As Trinity cannot be separated
Into parts dividing the unity
So love needs containing within passion
Not running carnally amok
Bridging what Greek describes
As individual characteristics
Components of the whole:
Our one word LOVE too easily
Erodes beyond the meaning meant.
In translation much more is lent.

John the Baptist

Repent, repent, the Kingdom's nigh
Turn back to your Lord on high.
Re-enter now the Promised Land
Receive those Blessings freely given
Salvation of souls is now at hand.
Serve God alone with conscience clear
Washing off all sin in Jordan River.
Soon will come the Spirit giver
Power from high to daunt all fear.
Come too the Kingdom of Heaven
Where God's will is done by all
Restoring the children of the fall.
Thus John the Baptist launched the way
That none from God might further stray.

Mary Magdalen

Many Marys made their mark
Not least the Magdalen, maid
Maybe mother, exposed and stark,
Sicut Lilium, recognition made
The garden of sorrows a delight,
Though Mark records they ran in fright,
To find her Lord restored for evermore.
Commissioned apostle news to tell
She has witnessed that all is well,
No need to go to Galilee shore.
Of her past there's so little we know
Save that she was a lady of means
Following the Lord where he might go
Supplying more than empty dreams.
Seven devils - who knows what kind?
Mary Magdalen restored in mind.

Appendix

The Hillside Parishes

March 1999

Parish Magazine Cover: Scaife Window

Parish Magazine Cover: Jesus before Pilate

An idea for an altar cross at Kir by Knowle
to be carved in wood.

Toddy 1994

Parish Magazine Cover: Figure proposed for an altar cross at Kirkby Knowle

Parish Magazine Cover: Tupping Time

Church teaching on marriage disregarded: a crisis of authority?

Sir, — The Revd Neil Patterson's article (Comment, 19 July) deserves a reply, because the Established Church needs to uphold and promote marriage as one of the building-blocks of society. Marriage has evolved, but Cranmer[1] laid a good foundation for its future. Not every prospective bride and groom may grasp the ins and outs of Bible poetry and theology when being prepared for their big day, but trying to get them to enter into seeing how they complete God's creativity in freely joining together once more what God in Adam and Eve originally divided does get some discussion going.

If the bride is on a me-me-me high and interested only in her procession, then the prognosis is not good. There was a wise old verger, when I was a curate, who would remark: "It won't last: they weren't with you." Sadly true, but from then more effort went into getting them with me.

Nevertheless, Mr Patterson overlooks, with a certain modesty, the fact that at some weddings the baby is already there and the big day might include a baptism. Perhaps this is nature's way into commitment?

Another good reason for the Church to promote marriage is that other religions, particularly Islam, are wanting when away from their cultural and home roots. Dazzled by the freedom of indigenous girls here, and frustrated by a system that keeps their own girls under lock and key, they have a problem that the recent convictions in Oxford of a group of girl-exploiters highlights.

Sex is here to stay, but, according to a Women's Hour programme that I had to listen to with my wife in the car, sex education is almost entirely lacking, because the parents assume that their daughter will be off and away to do it. Ignorance is not bliss; nor is endless intermarriage of cousins[2], judging by the remedial-surgery adverts.

Let the Church promote what is good and healthy, but stop the Church from invading every bedroom. The Roman Catholic Church still propounds its nonsense over contraception, which is a bit rich from a bundle of old bachelors. We should respect people's privacy, but let there be decent teaching for all about sex. The Prime Minister may be naive in saying that marriage is good for all, but if that is where the young generation is, then the Church must rise to the occasion.

I do not want to see same-sex marriage, but I have written a Service of Commitment for same- sex couples which cannot be hijacked into a wedding, as so often a service of prayer and thanksgiving for divorcees was.

Each generation interprets life and values as it sees them, sometimes alongside and sometimes in opposition to the generation that has reared it. The Church as an institution, with its rules and regulations, invasion of bedroom privacy, and antiquated laws that not even its clergy understand, plus the glare of publicity from abuse and exploitation by clergy themselves, is not attractive to the young. Romance is not dead, however, and a wedding is a start along a stimulating spiritual path for many. They, in turn, will tell others.

Church Times, August 9th, 2013

1. Cranmer was married and brought his wife back from Holland in a barrel.
2. Because of consanguinity especially amongst those of the Muslim faith producing genetic blood and kidney disorders some Gulf States have decreed that couples must have blood tests before marriage: should both couples have the dangerous gene they are discouraged from getting married or at least from having children.

Shooting

Early in January 2007 I was interviewed for *The Yorkshire Post* about government proposals to amend restrictions on shooting game on Sundays and other festivals alongside the abolition of game and game dealers licences. No one is aware of such recommendations I suspect! I think there are few who want to see Sunday further eroded, and probably no takers for a day's shooting on Christmas. More legislation that this government has not thought through - dreaming up ideas about things about which it has no experience nor knowledge. Certainly in shooting circles there is no desire for another day; six days are available and they are sufficient. It certainly makes a mockery of the Sabbath and its purpose. Added to which the countryside is crowded enough and it would be a shame to have too much on so that it has to be regulated. As it is there would be a clash over access, because at present the restriction prevents any clash with the walking and rambling fraternity and shooting syndicates as there is a complete day for the former when the latter are not out and about.

Yet it is thanks to Christianity and its legacy from Judaism that we have a week-end at all and a day that is special for other things. Re-creation, as Christian emphasis would put it, is our bonus and sadly it is only a few (the remnant as the Old Testament would say) who give God the glory first at some point in the day, or by special effort during the week. Many city churches do cater for evening and midday worship to enable people to open up their Sabbath back home for other activities that are legal. In anticipation of the Sabbath there have never been field sports on Sundays, nor indeed was there racing until commercial pressure forced the change. On the commercial issue about shooting on the Sabbath I hope gamekeepers and others, who help at the shoot by beating etc, will stand firm about keeping a day separate for the family and God. There are bound to be raised voices from a few who anticipate making more money out of the opportunity, but hopefully they will get no support from any workforce if the legislation does go ahead.

Country folk are probably more aware of the seven-day cycle with its Sabbath space and certainly my riding days with the army gave the horses rest on Sundays with minimum work in the stables for those of us on duty on that day. The Romans worked a system of a day off every ten and if we are not careful we will end up with a continuous stream of working days without even a breather unless employment contacts are alerted to the Christian provision for Sabbath rest. It is the case that Christianity has set a norm that now many walks of life challenge or, far worse, reject out of hand. Often this happens as a result of the work in hand having to maintain its momentum, rather like the blast furnaces in foundries having to run continuously until they were run done for maintenance and there was time off available.

Hillside Parishes Magazine, February 2007

A variation on this comes round again when others who do not appreciate the sport or the food want to ban shooting. Sadly greedy guns who treat lots of pheasants as feathered targets earn shooting a bad reputation. More so when they are not interested in eating what they shoot. There is, therefore, a strong case for limiting the number of pheasants that a shoot should release.

For more see The Sporting Gun *monthly magazine, February - April 2019 issues.*

A Full Life

As a sculptor I am used to dealing with three dimensions and thinking about ideas in 3D. The same is true of my ministry when it comes to encouraging people to live life in 3 dimensions: the physical and material: the mental: the spiritual. Half of marriage preparation is about helping people to look at life more fully. They will share the physical and the material; the bed and the pay packet. They will share the mental; ideas, hopes, joys, difficulties, planning etc. In offering their union to God they need to think in terms of sharing the spiritual side of life as well. The 3 Cs make up the 3D side, Companionship. communication and counselling on the spiritual level.

With that in mind I am attempting during Lent to look at A Full Life during our Wednesday evenings around the parish churches. On Ash Wednesday we will consider the Spiritual life. Vernon White from Lincoln Cathedral will lead us to consider Ageing. Then working back through the options and necessities of life we tackle The Single State (both single and widowed), With a Partner (within marriage and outside it), Growing Up, Back to the Beginning and on Maundy Thursday consider some of the personality clashes behind the passion story.

Far be it from me to disclose all my thoughts now for this Lent, but in working through the whole spectrum of life we can all call on our own experiences at sometime or another and be able to join in, whatever age we are. There are six stages but I will not attempt to colour code them! Life changes as much as colours do.

If we are to have a fuller life we need to look at how Christ can give us life more abundantly. We all want the best out of life. Well, there it is! John 10. (10-11) "I came that they may have life, and have it abundantly, I am the good shepherd." As John says, it is why he wrote the Gospel. 20 (31) 'these are written that you may believe that Jesus is the Christ, the Son of God, and that believing you may have life in his name.' In Christian terms we can measure what God does give us, even if we cannot satisfy the bank manager with it. In human terms we can deepen relationships and stretch ourselves outside of our selves. Our worst enemy is our self. Thus spiritually we can recognise and value in life that which makes it worth living, and which again in Christ is stretched beyond this life to promises of things greater beyond. Communion is about being together, living positively together to share our human resources and spiritual gifts and in itself is a foretaste of the heavenly banquet to come.

Hillside Parishes Magazine, March 1995

Horse to tractor

MENTION of Plough Sunday in Poet's Corner (19 January) brought back fond memories for the Revd Toddy Hoare, in Oxfordshire, who was serving the Hillside Parishes in North Yorkshire when an old horse-plough would be wheeled in for a special service of blessing put together by the Arthur Rank Centre.

"I had ploughed with horses in the village when a ploughing competition was held, and I had entered with my old grey Fergie and two-furrow plough all askew on the wrong settings. There was advice and help a-plenty, but the highlight was to plough some furrows with horses.

"One old parishioner told me: up at five to feed and ready the horse, set off at seven, start work at eight, a rest at ten, two hours' rest to feed the horse and lunch 12-2 p.m., off home at four, feed and groom the horse at five, home for a meal at six. A long day; and arms and back had to be sturdy, legs untiring."

Between Epiphany and Candlemas, or sometimes later, when ploughs used to go in, "the plough service was a welcome liturgical break of relevance, and attracted a few folk into the church." It also helped to focus minds on the Harvest Festival later in the year.

As chaplain, he was responsible for the Yorkshire Agricultural Society's Harvest Festival. "As it was one year in Selby Abbey, there was an old, polished Field Marshall tractor, as on my grandmother's farm. It didn't half rattle the stained-glass windows when it fired up," he says.

Churchwardens, be warned.

An item in editorial Features round-up in *The Church Times,* 23/2/18.

Ploughing with Horses

The harnessed horses bend necks to pull the plough,
Calling them on, my hands steadying the blade
Shearing and turning soil leaving enough
Furrow so one horse in lower trench bade,
T'other walked the length on higher firm ground.
This experience of a bygone age
Resurrected some familiar truths round
The ploughman who had companionship
With uncomplaining team, friendship,
Periods of rest, no engine straining rage,
While the tractor driver of today
Is a lone soul with radio on play
With many horse power against my two
Whose only falter may be loss of shoe.

Teapot Theology

What does a teapot suggest to you? If you treat it as a symbol it would be fair to say that it represents drink, refreshment, a welcome and hospitality. A quick search through the scriptures will enlarge upon those ideas. Drink: from many references I will choose three.

Proverbs 25.v21. 'if your enemy is hungry, give him bread to eat; and if he is thirsty, give him water to drink; for you will heap coals of lire upon his head, and the Lord will reward you." This idea is picked up in the sermon on the mount, Matt.5.v44. If we change enemy to stranger and think of coals of fire as indebtedness we arrive at basic hospitality as encountered all round the globe. This in turn is at the heart of the culture of the Middle East, though many would begin to doubt it in the present climate of terror.

Matt 11.vv 18-19. There is a contrast between Jesus and John the Baptist in their attitudes to drink and the public perception of them at the time. No doubt the teapot would represent John quite well in this instance! Luke 12. vv 13-34. Here we have a discourse by Jesus on life in general and how we might approach it better and more healthily, for drink is part of daily life and the teapot can represent that too.

Next we can move onto the sacraments but the chalice as a receptacle becomes the better symbol as my teapot is the container, so to speak, from which the refreshment is initially poured. John 6. 55, "My blood is drink indeed" raises the metaphor to the status of sacrament but the meaning is clear that it is to feed us on the spiritual level. But let us stay with John a bit, for when Jesus encounters the woman of Samaria in chapter 4 he may well have demanded a cup of tea in our culture this day and age to refresh himself. However it would not be out of place to continue in verse 13 to talk about living water to negate drinking and imbibe eternal life instead. Again in John 7.37, Jesus refers to himself and his teaching as the living water when a libation of water was poured on the altar each day for

8 days at the Feast of Tabernacles. This was to commemorate life in the wilderness when God provided water from the rock, but now Jesus said "If anyone thirst, let him come to me and drink". My teapot now contains real substance!

Another realm I would like to visit through the tardis of my teapot is prayer. The teapot is a good symbol when we come to the Celtic prayer A Rune of Hospitality. It goes "I saw a stranger today. I put food for him in the eating-place And drink in the drinking-place And music in the listening-place".

Hillside Parishes Magazine.

England, home and beauty

From Christmas, and during the Epiphany period, we think about the "word became flesh and dwelt (tented or tabernacled) amongst us" (John 1, v.14). So what are we to do during Lent and Easter? It is the time for encouraging God to be "at home" in us. In other words, the spirit that brooded over the emptiness of God's creation fills us if we open up, just as God's spirit fills the rest of creation. Healing and wholeness come from this when the Spirit fills us. (By healing we need to understand that in the case of chronic or terminal illness reconciliation takes place: an aspect of healing whereby we have the grace to live and cope with what we have got.)

Would the media have heard better before condemning? To sit at the Archbishop of Canterbury's feet in February was a good eye-opener. He amended his talk from the Friday to say, on the Saturday, that the term "at home in" better describes our opening up and letting God into ourselves - rather than the term "inhabiting". Lent becomes a good time to home in on this and cultivate that open-ness. Communion is part of this. Rather than the flesh and blood of Christ, which we take on board and digest, there should be more a sense of us becoming the flesh and blood of God. God becomes present through us.

As a sculptor, especially a portrait sculptor, the Archbishop struck a particular chord with me. He talked about empty faces that expressed nothing. As vehicles of the heavenly body in this life, we need to radiate Christ, to express Him. Scars, smiles, wrinkles are all part of Him in our lives. Someone said, of a bust that I did of David Jenkins: "A life well lived". The clown, Roly Bain, expresses the same in a different way, with an impishness and face paint - the painted clown.

And the purpose of this being God filled, being "at home with" God? To glorify God, to be God centred, to worship God. Without the Spirit we have not the strength for it. As Jesus said of the blind man he healed in the Temple (John 9, v. 1-12): He was not born blind out of sin but to better glorify and express God. Rowan Williams' starting point was Matthew 12 v.43-45: how the unclean spirit, swept from a man, returns with seven other spirits worse than before if the empty space has not been better filled. Lent is not about sweeping out and doing spiritual spring cleaning, but making room for and encouraging more Holy Spirit. May your Lent be useful and may we help you fill up not be fed up!

Hillside Parishes Magazine, March 2003

Article on Snow Prin, Oxford Mail, 24/1/1979.

Faithful image

There was always a danger that sculptor Toddy Hoare might get a frosty reception from the Rev. Jim Hickinbotham when he discovered this effigy in the gardens of Wycliffe Hall.

But Toddy, a second year student at the Oxford theological college, was keeping a cool head and hoping his painstaking work would melt the college principal's heart.

He completed his first work in snow — named Snow Prin — in just 40 minutes, with the help of a banker's card and a bunch of keys. "The principal's wife recognised it straight away, " he said, "and so did everyone else I think. " Now he plans to preserve the work in a deep freeze and present it to the principal on his retirement at the end of the academic year.

Picture: Athar Chaudhry

Letter to the Times, published on 6th February 2008; Re Clergy Training. "Who pays to train the Clergy?"

Dear Sir,

All your published letters on this subject today (2/2/08) are very negative. Theology is not a mere study of comparative religion but an approach to a subject with dedication. We clergy are often the only ones around after comfortable working hours to help folk or bring solace to troubled lives. Yes, something beyond ourselves motivates us and we enjoy a peace from finding a deeper meaning in our lives. The first careers of both my wife and myself before ordination are very much part of our ongoing ministries, as indeed was my second career when I retraced my steps as an army padre. If people put more value on what they benefit from for free at all hours and in all stages of their lives, and if our heritage of fine buildings did not consume so much of our freewill offerings, maybe we could afford more second degrees, but for the present we give up much to serve others.

Yours faithfully,
TH.

CPSIA information can be obtained
at www.ICGtesting.com
Printed in the USA
BVHW071121060319
541923BV00015B/943/P